# ART DECO

## A GUIDE FOR COLLECTORS

# ART DECO
## A GUIDE FOR
## COLLECTORS

Katharine Morrison McClinton

 Clarkson N. Potter, Inc./Publishers  NEW YORK

DISTRIBUTED BY CROWN PUBLISHERS, INC.

*Published by Clarkson N. Potter, Inc., 225 Park Avenue South, New York, New York 10003.*

*CLARKSON N. POTTER, POTTER, and colophon are trademarks of Clarkson N. Potter, Inc.*

*Manufactured in the United States of America.*

*Library of Congress Catalog Card Number: 76–187511*

*ISBN 0-517-54599-3*

10 9 8 7 6 5 4 3 2 1

*First Revised Edition*

# Acknowledgments

My acknowledgments go back to 1928 when on my second trip to Paris I met the late Léon Deshairs, Conservateur de la Bibliothèque du Musée des Arts Décoratifs, for whose aid I remain grateful. I also owe sincere thanks to each one of the great Art Deco designers: Emile-Jacques Ruhlmann, Maurice Dufrène, Djo-Bourgeois, Puiforcat, Paul Poiret and many others who gave freely of their time for personal interviews.

And now, forty years later, my special thanks go to Elayne Varian, Finch College Museum Director, Contemporary Wing, and to her assistant, Dianne D. Hausserman.

I am also deeply grateful to Mrs. Pat Carter of the Antiques Center of America and to the following dealers there: Barry Friedman, Carol Ferranti, Gladys Koch, Fred Silberman, Robert Morgan, Frank Weston and Betty Lipton who allowed me to study their stocks and who often provided valuable information. Still another thank-you is due Roy Blakey for the excellent black-and-white photographs of articles at the Antiques Center of America.

I wish to thank Mrs. Elizabeth Usher, Chief Librarian of the Metropolitan Museum of Art, and her efficient staff; and the staff of the Art and Architecture reference room of the New York Public Library. I also appreciate the assistance of Janet Thorpe, Associate Curator of Decorative Arts, Cooper-Hewitt Museum of Design; Mrs. Lillian Nassau; Kevin Tierney and Ronald de Silva of Parke-Bernet Galleries; Jane Schadel, Corning Museum of Glass, and Patricia Robert, Radio City Music Hall; Theodora Morgan, Managing Editor, *National Sculpture Review*, and D. Wayne Johnson, Medallic Art Company.

# CONTENTS

PREFACE                                                          ix

1  COLLECTING ART DECO                                            3

2  WHAT IS ART DECO?                                              6

3  FURNITURE                                                     13

4  RUGS AND TEXTILES                                             61

5  CLOCKS, LIGHTING FIXTURES AND LAMPS                           81

6  POTTERY AND PORCELAIN                                        103

7  GLASS                                                        127

8  SILVER                                                       156

9  BRONZE AND OTHER METAL
     STATUETTES AND MEDALLIONS                                  185

10  GRAPHICS AND POSTERS                                        211

11  JEWELRY, COMPACTS, PURSES
      AND CIGARETTE LIGHTERS                                    245

12  KITSCH                                                      263

BIBLIOGRAPHY                                                    271

INDEX                                                          273

*Color insert follows page 150.*

# PREFACE

I WAS IN PARIS IN 1925 AND VISITED THE EXPOSITION DES ARTS DECORATIFS et Industriels Modernes when the new style, then referred to as Art Décoratif, or Art Moderne, was reviewed and celebrated. I was also in Paris in 1928 and visited the Salon des Artistes Décorateurs of that year. At that time I met and personally interviewed the important ensembliers and designers. Léon Deshairs, then Conservateur de la Bibliothèque du Musée des Arts Décoratifs, gave me valuable information and placed at my disposal the French references on modern French decorative arts. Later he wrote the introduction for my book, *Modern French Decoration*, which was published by G. P. Putnam's in 1930.

The Exposition des Arts Décoratifs in 1925 presented styles that filled the years from the end of Art Nouveau to the rise of the Bauhaus. It was the style of art between the two world wars. The exhibits introduced a new style in the field of decorative arts. They represented the work of architects, cabinetmakers, metalworkers and textile designers as well as products from many other fields of decorative art. Painters and sculptors not only exhibited their works but also cooperated in the design of minor art objects. The sculptor Antoine

Bourdelle designed doorknobs and well-known painters designed rugs, tapestries and upholstery materials.

This modern decorative art was presented by the decorators, or ensembliers, in Salon exhibitions from 1925 to 1935, with the emphasis on interior decoration, furniture, rugs, drapery and upholstery materials. However, lighting fixtures and accessories, such as pottery, glass and bronze figures, were also displayed with each interior. The impact of the movement was so great that designers in all fields, including those of silverware and jewelry, were swept into the stream.

Not all art of the 1920s and 1930s is Art Deco, and not all Art Deco has the same characteristics. Early Art Deco has graceful, feminine forms, and later examples are characterized by cubist forms. There are the refined products of such artists as Ruhlmann, Puiforcat and Mallet-Stevens, and there are the kitsch mass-produced products in plastic and chrome designed for the general public.

It was not until 1966 that the title Art Deco was given to the style. Although Art Deco is a catchy term it is not altogether satisfactory because it puts the emphasis on the popular jazz phase of the style and the cheap commercial kitsch, or trashy, product. This side of Art Deco was never accepted by the French designers. It was not shown in the 1925 Exhibition and never appeared in the annual exhibitions of the Salons, nor was it illustrated in the decorative art journals of the period.

I lived through the era of the Roaring Twenties—of the saxophone, the raccoon coat, black lace stockings, feather fans and the Stutz Bearcat. It was the age of Zelda and Scott Fitzgerald, but I was there too —and so was Gertrude Stein. Many of the artists that I met in 1925 and 1928, including Maurice Dufrène, Ruhlmann and Paul Poiret, would be shocked and indignant if they knew that their work was dubbed "Art Deco."

# ART DECO

## A GUIDE FOR COLLECTORS

# 1

# COLLECTING
# ART DECO

ART DECO OBJECTS OF THE 1920S AND 1930S ARE TODAY CLASSED AS serious antiques, yet they were neither produced nor collected from 1940 on. It was not until after the commemorative exhibition "Les Années '25" at the Musée des Arts Décoratifs in 1966 that there was any real interest in this art form. In the years since that nostalgic exhibition a few pioneer collectors began searching for and finding articles by the famous-name designers of the period, and in the process transferred their interest from Art Nouveau to Art Deco. Indeed, Art Nouveau has now been almost totally eclipsed by Art Deco. Shops specializing in Art Deco have opened in Paris, London and New York, and museums too have turned their attention to Art Deco resulting in exhibitions both in Europe and in America. The first such exhibition in this country was at the Finch College Museum in November 1970, and the Minneapolis Institute of Art devoted eleven of their large galleries to an exhibition of Art Deco in July 1971.

Art Deco items, especially glass, ceramics and bronze statuettes, have come up in recent auctions in Paris, at Christie's and Sotheby's in London and at Parke Bernet in New York, where top designer pieces are selling often for several thousand dollars.

Today Art Deco is the talk of the town. It is again racing across the fashion scene. Plays on Broadway are often set with scenery and costumes in Art Deco style, and television productions are also influenced by the flashy colors and geometric motifs of the style. Art Deco competes with Art Nouveau in the decoration of popular restaurants and night spots in New York. The jagged geometric design of the Chrysler Building and the inside decorations of Radio City Music Hall—both examples of Art Deco style—are looked at with new interest these days.

What of Art Deco for the collector? Only a few names interest those in the know. In glass the most famous name is René Lalique, but glass by such artists as François Décorchemont, Antoine Daum, Maurice Marinot, Jean Luce, Argy-Rousseau and Henri Navarre are also in higher-bracket collecting. Furniture by name designers is expensive, but there are several shops in New York that have collections for all. Top names in pottery include René Buthaud, Emile Decoeur, Emile Lenoble and Jean Mayodon, as well as the ceramics of the Wiener Werkstätte designers. In silver, it is Jean Puiforcat, Josef Hoffmann, Dagobert Peche and Laparra. The enamel vases of Jean Dunand, Claudius Linossier and C. Fauré are also in the list of expensive, museum-quality Art Deco items now in New York shops.

There is also a lot of good Art Deco around at reasonable prices, and there are still a few sleepers, such as signed Robj porcelain figures. There are perfume bottles, small lamps, figurines and costume jewelry, enamel cigarette cases, compacts and lighters, and pieces of decorated china and glassware. The bulk of these articles can still be found at moderate prices in today's antique shops. Since Art Deco was a mass-produced as well as a custom-made style, and since it appeared in practically all industrial and graphic arts media, there are quantities of articles.

The collector should decide on a theme or an item that holds his interest, and concentrate his collection on that item, since specialization always pays. Also, now is the time to set standards and look for the best and hopefully choose objects that will continue to hold interest and increase in value as the years go by. Although collectors of the future may not have the zeal of the present-day collector of Art Deco, there are items of fine design and elegance that are unique and pleasing enough to find a permanent place along with similar objects of earlier styles.

Besides custom-made designer pieces, there are anonymous and mass-produced pieces that are good examples of the style. If the collector is interested in objects for laughs, Art Deco mass-produced ashtrays, bookends, nude statuettes imitating ancient bronzes and plastic jewelry are in abundance. Though not art, these knickknacks catch the spirit of Art Deco and the jazz phase of the 1920s. This kind of collecting is fun, but it gives a distorted picture of the age as a whole and is a misrepresentation of the decorative art of the 1920s and 1930s, which drew inspiration from serious art movements such as Futurism and Cubism, and was also influenced by the Bauhaus.

# 2 WHAT IS ART DECO?

ART DECO IS A CLASSICAL, SYMMETRICAL, RECTILINEAR STYLE. IT DEVELOPED and thrived in the years between 1910 and 1935 reaching its high point between 1925 and 1935. It was originally known as Art Moderne; the name Art Deco is a shortening of the title of the first international display of objects in the style—the Exposition Internationale des Arts Décoratifs et Industriels Modernes—held in Paris in 1925. However, this exhibition was not fully representative of the modern movement, for although the decorative arts of numerous countries were shown, that of France alone was comprehensive. The Weimar Bauhaus and Dutch de Stijl, both important influences in modern design, were ignored.

Throughout the Art Deco period there was great diversity and a restless search for direction—the revival of craftsmanship and the individual expression of the artist, on the one hand; the group movements, such as the German Werkbunds and the Wiener Werkstätte of Vienna, on the other hand. Also the custom-made and the mass-produced product were both important expressions of the Art Deco style.

The roots of Art Deco lie in the austere side of Art Nouveau. Early in the twentieth century there had been evidences of a revolt against the exaggerated curves and asymmetrical forms of Art Nouveau. The movement in protest against the sweetness and fantasy of Art Nouveau began in England with Charles F. A. Voysey and Charles Rennie Mackintosh. Both these men had a feeling for the vertical line, which was later to influence the use of the straight line and geometrical forms of Josef Hoffmann in Vienna. The theories of the German architects Otto Wagner and Adolf Loos were the inspiration of the de Stijl group of Holland and the German Bauhaus. The French architects A. and G. Perret led the French reaction against Art Nouveau. Robert Mallet-Stevens and Pierre Chareau also refused to conform to the fanciful curves of Art Nouveau, and their work shows an awareness of modern materials. The American architects Louis Sullivan and Frank Lloyd Wright attempted to integrate furniture and objects into their architectural environment. All these architectural secessionists were the true pioneers of Art Deco, but there were many more concrete evidences at work.

The Ballets Russes in Paris in 1909 really marked the beginning of the Art Deco style, and Léon Bakst's striking Oriental designs and bold exotic colors had great impact on the decorative arts of the period. This influence continued unabated until the outbreak of the war in 1914. Such ballets as the *Firebird, Petrushka, L'Après-midi d'un Faune* and *Le Coq d'Or* not only made a great contribution to the theater but also increased the importance of the painter and influenced such French designers as Paul Iribe. The painters André Drésa, Georges Desvallières, André Dunoyer de Segonzac, Robert Bonfils and Francis Jourdain were also commissioned to design sets for dramas and operas. From 1917 French painters were commissioned to work with the Ballets Russes. These included Georges Braque, André Derain, Juan Gris, Marie Laurencin, Matisse and Picasso. Thus, the public was initiated into Futurism, Expressionism, Cubism and other art movements by way of the theater. All these art movements played an important part in the development of Art Deco.

The foundations of Art Deco had been established before the outbreak of the First World War, and Art Deco had become a fully developed conscious style by the time the war had ended. Art Deco attracted many fine craftsmen and, with a complete line of decorative objects of related and harmonizing design available, the Art Deco style emerged as a coordinated whole.

Modern artists sought to create and establish an art expressive of their times. This meant the acceptance of speed and intensity and a breakdown of traditional patterns. The speed of the car, the locomotive, and especially the airplane, changed the way of seeing objects, and this brought about changes in their form and design. For example, the backward diagonal lines of the racing car following the direction of its movement is one of the characteristics of Art Deco line. Speed and dynamics are also characteristics of the engine, and the machine became an inspiration to many artists, its influence resulting in an intensity of color and force of line and form. To capture the eye of the speeding passerby line was made simpler, forms bolder, and color purer and more intense.

In 1922/23 the opening of Tutankhamen's tomb produced an effect on designers similar to that of the discovery of Pompeii and Herculaneum in the eighteenth century and of Napoleon's Egyptian campaign in the early nineteenth century. The Egyptian influence was particularly noticeable in the decorative arts and in jewelry, although architecture borrowed motifs for doorways and entrances, and movie theaters in both America and England were redecorated in the Egyptian manner. Pierre Legrain designed a chair of palmwood veneer in the Egyptian style. A ladies' writing desk of lacquer with stepped drawers made in 1920–25 is also in the Musée des Arts Décoratifs in Paris. A stylized palm-tree floor lamp by Eliel Saarinen again shows the Egyptian influence. Saarinen also designed palmette-inlaid cabinets and chairs. However, the effect that Egyptian motifs had on furniture and interior decoration of the twenties was slight; none was noticeable in the objects displayed in the 1925 Exposition. But the shapes of the pyramid and the scarab motif, hieroglyphics and the use of Egyptian colors in enamel and semiprecious stones are seen especially in jewelry. Sphinx heads were mounted on marble clocks, sculptors produced bronze figures of Egyptian cats, and figures of Cleopatra are seen on bronze and pottery inkwells. Some of the most beautiful designs of Egyptian inspiration are seen in the costumes of Erté for the *Sphinx* (1924) and the *Nile* (1925) ballets.

The influence of the Indian cultures of North and South America was felt in the arts in the late 1920s and early 1930s. Chamber of commerce trips were organized to Mexico City and some went as far south as Chichén Itzá and Yucatán. Novelists wrote books about Mexico and Mexican art was featured in exhibitions throughout

America. Paul Frankl designed furniture in stepped skyscraper forms and set pots of cacti on tables and shelves. Erté's "Indian Dagger Dance" curtain for *George White's Scandals* in 1928 was inspired by the Indian designs of the Southwest. But it was the countries of Brazil and Peru that had the greatest effect on European art. The stepped forms of Aztec temples and the materials of Indian art—obsidian, onyx, rock crystal and jade—became popular for jewelry; sculptors made bronze figures of Amazons and Indians.

Exhibitions of African Negro art in Paris in the 1920s brought the forms and motifs of still another culture to the notice of designers. The masks and native sculpture of the French Congo became an important influence not only in the painting of the Cubists but in the design, color and texture of the rugs of Da Silva Bruhns and the fabrics of Rodier. Animal skins were used as upholstery and even applied as coverings for cabinets and chests.

The huge tropical leaf patterns of printed cottons were also inspired by African art. Erté's curtain for the African Ballet in the *George White's Scandals* of 1924 is an excellent example of the influence of African design. In the 1920s everything Negro came into fashion— jazz music and dances including the black bottom, the charleston and the turkey trot.

The school or group was an important influence in the decorative art of the 1920s. In order to promote modern decorative art, French artists worked together in groups in imitation of similar groups in Germany, Austria and Holland. On the eve of World War I an association of young artists in Paris, led by André Mare was formed. They chose the basket and garland of fruits and flowers as the symbol of their new style. This became a favorite motif with such traditional French designers such as Paul Follot and André Groult. The tendency toward a collective effort rather than an individual one grew stronger after the war. In 1919 the group that Mare started founded the Compagnie des Arts Français (Sue et Mare). Other workshops were formed, mainly in the department stores of Paris. The most important department store ateliers were Primavera at Au Printemps, directed by Mme Gauchet-Guillard; La Maîtrise at Galeries Lafayette, directed by Maurice Dufrène; Pomone at Bon Marché, directed by Paul Follot, the Studium at the Louvre, directed by Etienne Kohlmann and Maurice Matet. René Joubert founded Décoration Intérieure Moderne known as DIM. These workshops designed not only furniture but the complete interior. They employed a large group of designers and produced a full line of decorative arts including rugs, draperies, upholstery materials, lamps, lighting fixtures, china, glass and metalwares. This group effort not only helped establish the style but it gave support to artists who might not have made it alone.

In the 1925 Exposition all these shops had individual pavilions for their displays. Emile-Jacques Ruhlmann had his own exhibit, "Le Pavillon d'un Collectionneur." The 1925 exhibits were essentially French and unmistakably twentieth century. The interesting factor, however, was the individuality and diversity, since both the work of traditional designers like Maurice Dufrène, Ruhlmann, Paul Follot, Sue et Mare and Léon Jallot was shown, as well as that of the moderns —Mallet-Stevens, Kohlmann, Djo-bourgeois and René Herbst. Nevertheless, this 1925 Exposition marked the end of traditional influences and the beginning of the union between art and industry.

In 1928 Pierre Chareau, René Herbst, Francis Jourdain and Robert Mallet-Stevens founded the Union des Artistes Modernes that became influential in directing the course of French decorative design in the 1930s. In each annual exhibition of the Salon des Artistes Décorateurs from that year on through the 1930s one sees the gradual acceptance of functional forms and the use of the materials of modern industry. Although there were differences between the Art Deco of the 1920s and that of the 1930s, the change was not an abrupt one.

As I've already said, not all decorative art of the 1920s and 1930s is Art Deco. Also, there are two different types of Art Deco: The graceful curvilinear type best expressed by such designers as Paul Follot and René Lalique; the functional machine-inspired type practiced by such young designers as Djo-bourgeois. One phase of Art Deco was tied to the rhythm of the times as reflected in the ballet and the designs of Bakst, Erté and Paul Iribe. This produced a gay, fanciful style but one that was still based on genuine values.

By 1928 the graceful femininity of Art Deco and the motifs of design —the geometric rose, the garlands and baskets of flowers, fountains and jets of water, doves, female deer and nudes—were decidedly on the decline. Cubism became the dominant influence, and the new young designers favored the stark simplicity, austerity and innovations of modern life and industry. Curves gave way to angularity and motifs of design tended to be more dynamic. Figures were shown in straining positions with outstretched hands and streaming hair. The sun's rays cut through the sky and clouds raced in the wind. Lightning bolts, greyhounds, automobiles and airplanes, which exemplified speed, were popular motifs. The following description of Art Deco, circa 1930, is taken from *Modern French Decorative Art* (second series), by Léon Deshairs: "Light, glistening rustless steel furniture, and soft and mysterious lighting effects—obtained by refraction or diffusion—which entail a minimum of visible fittings and cumbersome supports, typify the taste of 1930. . . . The novelty does not consist in the use of metal, but in the fact that never before has it penetrated so boldly into the most luxurious and fastidious of homes. In the office suites, the private bars, the dining and living-rooms shown at the Spring and Autumn Paris Salons of 1928 and 1929, strip-metal and metal-tubing—used in conjunction with wood or glass and even adapting itself quite naturally to the forms of chairs, settees, etc., covered with leather, or various materials in assorted colours—were everywhere in evidence. . . . Today the decorator frankly borrows all the motifs he can from industry."

This change in fashion and the trend to austerity gradually won acceptance and by the mid-1930s rectilinear forms had completely taken over, and new synthetic materials—plywood and metal tubing —and the machine crowded out traditional materials and crafts. Marble and metal used in their raw and unworked state became time-savers.

Cubistic geometry was the most important influence in Art Deco. This abstract phase of Art Deco was exercised by such craftsmen as Ruhlmann in furniture and interiors; Lalique, Daum and Marinot in glass; Jean Dunand in lacquers and metals; Edgar Brandt and Raymond Subes in ironwork; Puiforcat in silver; and Jean Fouquet in jewelry. These artists produced the outstanding Art Deco of the period in France.

Although Art Deco was a French style, it was not confined to France. In fact it produced quite as full an expression in Germany and Austria, although the decorative arts of both these countries remained under the cloud of two wars. The language barrier, and the lack of any general distribution of books and periodicals illustrating the decorative arts of these countries during the 1920s and 1930s, has kept the public in ignorance of the many interesting products from such centers of art production as the Austrian Wiener Werkstätte and the German Werkbunds, and it is only within recent years that they are getting their full recognition. If we are to see the complete picture of Art Deco it is necessary to sweep away prejudice and study the style as expressed in both Germany and Austria as well as in other countries during the 1920s and 1930s. Modern German and Austrian painters and sculptors of the period are recognized for their contribution to the art world, but the fine craftsmanship of the cabinetmakers, goldsmiths, silversmiths and other decorative artists of the period has not been given the attention it deserves. Research in the decorative arts magazines, such as *Deutsche Kunst und Dekoration* and *Die Kunst*, both of which publications continued without interruption to be published, give a picture of Art Deco as expressed in these countries.

Art Deco is now a historical style. It was the first style to make modernism popular with an audience large enough to allow for mass production. Yet, it was this mass production that led the style astray and distorted it so that today its faults are emphasized rather than its true values. The style as a whole is only spurious and insincere to those who look in that direction rather than at the true values and serious aims that were the ideals of the designers.

# 3 FURNITURE

THE FURNITURE OF THE 1920s REFLECTED THE CHANGES IN FASHION AND style and was related to the new architecture and to the new materials. The furniture designers were, however, divided into two groups: the traditionalists who tried to adapt the forms and techniques of the past to the demands of modern life and the innovators who rejected the past and accepted the materials and possibilities of the modern machine.

The traditionalists disliked the uncompromising use of the straight line and favored the curve. They claimed that beauty should have a place aside from usefulness and that delicate color should have a place in every interior. The traditionalists produced furniture of fine workmanship and rich materials. They used mahogany, rosewood, elm, sycamore and walnut and fruitwoods, such as cherry, almond, palm, apricot and pear for inlay. Exotic woods, including ebony, thuga, macassar, amboina, amaranth, palisander and satinwood, were used to give richness of color to the plain, shiny satinlike surfaces that were usually devoid of any carving. The beauty of the natural grain and pattern of the woods also added to the surface richness. Lacquer was

Mirror with wooden frame decorated with gilt Art Deco motifs and silk tassels. *Frank Weston and Robert Morgan, The Antiques Center of America*

used by such decorators as Maison Martine and ivory inlay, mother-of-pearl and tortoiseshell also gave added ornamentation. Drawer handles were made of ivory, bronze or silk tassels, and plaques of bronze, silver or ivory decorated the fronts of cabinets. Marble was often used for tops of cabinets and was available in many colors: black, gray, green, Carrara red, and orange yellow, as well as in flowery brocaded patterns.

The furniture of traditionalist designers varied with each individual craftsman:

Léon Jallot, a traditionalist, was the first to introduce nails of ivory and bronze into the construction and decoration of modern furniture. In making his furniture Jallot used both native and foreign woods and enhanced their beauty by arranging the natural grain of the wood to form the decoration. This is the outstanding characteristic of his furniture. He also used multicolored and gold lacquers, and since he was also a wood-carver he often used carved borders.

Palisander wood cabinet with marble top. Léon Jallot, 1928. *From* Modern French Decoration *by Katharine Morrison Kahle (McClinton)*

Green and gold lacquer mirror. Designed by Sue et Mare, decorated by Paul Véra, circa 1920. *The Metropolitan Museum of Art, Edward C. Moore, Jr., Gift Fund, 1923*

Gold lacquer screen. Léon Jallot, circa 1927. *From* Art et Décoration, *1929*

Maurice Dufrène, a traditionalist, created sumptuous feminine interiors in the traditional manner, but since he was connected with the workshop at Galeries Lafayette he was swayed by public taste, and his later work was quite revolutionary.

Paul Follot was a traditionalist whose work is characterized by delicate colors and graceful curves. He was fond of marquetry, lacquer, bronze plaques and carving. He stood against the introduction of industrial features into house decoration.

Sue et Mare: The Compagnie des Arts Français was founded by Louis Sue and André Mare in 1919. They designed interiors and all sorts of decorative objects to furnish them. Other designers working with them included Desvallières, Charles Dufresne, Maurice Marinot, Gustave Jaulmes and Paul Véra. Their furniture design was adapted from the Louis Philippe period and was curvilinear and decorated with lacquer, veneer and carved wood details.

Commode. Designed by Sue et Mare, decorated by Paul Véra, circa 1920. *The Metropolitan Museum of Art, Edward C. Moore, Jr., Gift Fund, 1923*

Chair with carved basket of flowers and leaves, and tassels. Louis Sue, circa 1920. *The Metropolitan Museum of Art, Edward C. Moore, Jr., Gift Fund, 1923*

André Groult based his work on traditional forms and a love of ample curvilinear forms enhanced with Art Deco motifs—baskets of flowers, ropes, tassels and feathers. Paintings by Marie Laurencin were usually seen in his interiors.

Emile-Jacques Ruhlmann was the great traditionalist. He created for a wealthy clientele. His furniture was characterized by perfect workmanship and the use of rare and exotic woods—purple amaranth, palisander and violet wood, and macassar ebony enriched with ivory and bronze plaques, marble and morocco leather. In his "Pavillon d'un Ambassadeur" in the 1925 Paris Exposition, the huge cabinet set on a block base had a stringing border of ivory and ivory drawer knobs. A recess in the center of the cabinet held a small bronze figure of a nude woman.

Ruhlmann's interiors had a richness and luxury not found in the work of other decorators. His massive elegant cabinets often have delicate curved spindle legs. All the ornamentation is subordinate to the fine proportion and gracefulness of the whole. Ruhlmann had definite ideas about the furniture design of the 1920s. When I visited his studio in 1928 he wrote the following in my notebook: "The modern style employs pure forms dictated by reason, beautiful proportion of volumes and elegance and directness of line. Added to these are beautiful inlays of precious materials and plaques of bronze, silver or ivory."

Walnut dining room extension table and gondola chairs. Emile-Jacques Ruhlmann, 1925 Paris Exposition. *Lent by Lillian Nassau, Ltd., for the Finch College Museum Art Deco Exhibition, 1970*

Cabinet with bronze plaque and marble top. Emile-Jacques Ruhlmann, 1928.
*From* Modern French Decoration *by Katharine Morrison Kahle (McClinton)*

In contrast to the traditionalists the rationalist innovators chose the straight line as the line of beauty and regarded furniture as a part of interior architecture. They simplified line, form and decoration, and chose modern materials such as metal, leather and tile.

Djo-bourgeois was one of the foremost rationalists. He was an architect, and the force and techniques of the architect are seen in his furniture. He was a master of plane and volume and much of his furniture was built in as a part of the interior architecture. The pieces are constructed of simple wood, metal and marble. In 1928 Djo-bourgeois wrote in my notebook: "The furniture is very simple and should be a part of architecture. Forms should correspond to their purpose. Everything ought to be practical, nothing unuseful."

Pierre Chareau, a rationalist, was working before 1920. He was one of the first to use plastics, although he preferred fine materials such as mahogany and rosewood. He used volumes and planes to create audacious and severe furniture without any added ornament.

Bookcase cabinet. Pierre Chareau, 1928. *From* Modern French Decoration *by Katharine Morrison Kahle (McClinton)*

Small table with marble top. Pierre
Chareau. *From* Art et Décoration,
*1923*

Walnut combination piece. Pierre Chareau. *From* Modern French Decoration
*by Katharine Morrison Kahle (McClinton)*

Living room of California apartment of Templeton Crocker. Designed by Jean-Michel Frank, 1929. *From* Modern French Decoration *by Katharine Morrison Kahle (McClinton)*

Jean-Michel Frank created interiors devoid of ornament and color except for the natural tones of wood, leather, straw and natural unbleached fabrics, yet the final effect is one of luxury. In 1929 Frank furnished a room in the apartment of Templeton Crocker in San Francisco, California.

René Herbst was a radical. He designed furniture adapted to its function, and used wood, steel and aluminum without any added ornamentation.

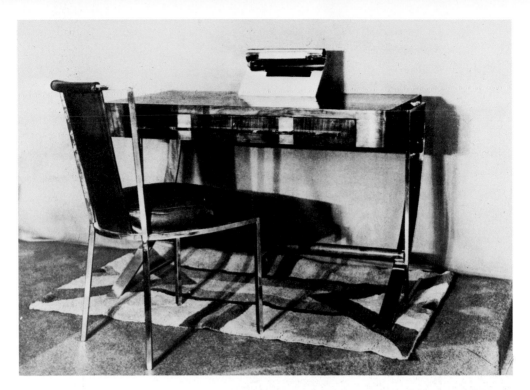

Lady's writing table. René Herbst. *From* Modern
French Decorative Art *by Léon Deshairs*

Etienne Kohlmann was the youngest of the radicals. He received his
training at l'Ecole Boulle and was a builder as well as a designer of
furniture. His furniture is simple and without added decoration. In the
1929 Salon he exhibited a bedroom with a bed and table combined in
one piece.

Brilliant color and bold floral and leaf designs characterize the
interiors of Martine founded by Paul Poiret. Floral motifs, such as
roses, daisies, fuchsias, bachelor's buttons, ferns and large leaves, are
treated in the manner of peasant art. Color is everywhere, in the
draperies, rugs and accessories, and even the furniture is lacquered in
colorful floral designs or in gold or silver. The walls are often covered
with colored inlay of wood-shavings. Floral carpets also set a style
imitated by other designers. Poiret himself was a couturier and costume designer but a visit to Austria interested him in the work of the
Wiener Werkstätte, and in 1912, he established Martine, a school of
decorative art, and later, with the aid of such painters as Raoul Dufy,
Foujita, Paul Iribe and Mario Simon, he created interiors. The private
dining room created by Martine for the *Ile-de-France* in 1927 had
lacquered furniture, walls of tropical leaf design and a matching rug.

Amboina wood commode with ivory inlay and
drawer handles, and marble top. Jules Leleu,
French, circa 1925. *The Metropolitan Museum of
Art, Gift of Miss Agnes Miles Carpenter, 1946*

Other well-known designers who exhibited in the annual Salon
des Artistes Décorateurs included René Joubert, Jules-Emile Leleu,
Dominique, Maurice Matet, Charlotte Perriand, J. J. Adnet, André
Fréchet, Louis Sognot, René Gabriel, Henri Rapin, and in 1928/30, L.
Alavoine. The most radical designers were a new group formed by Le
Corbusier, Pierre Jeannert, Mies van der Röhe and Charlotte Perriand.
Their tables and chairs of tubing, metal and glass were manufactured
by Thonet in Germany.

Although the furniture of the various designers had individual
characteristics there were certain elements that tied them to the period
as a whole. Also, the furniture as a whole was in harmony with its
setting since the designer of the furniture was usually the designer, if
not the architect, of the interior.

Boudoir. Louis Sognot, 1928. *From* Modern French Decoration *by Katharine Morrison Kahle (McClinton)*

The Ethel and Raymond Worgelt Study, 575 Park Avenue, New York City. Designed by Alavoine, 1928–1930. *Courtesy The Brooklyn Museum, Gift of Raymond Worgelt*

a

b

d

Armchairs: (a) Emile-Jacques Ruhlmann; (b) Léon Bouchet; (c) René Joubert; (d) Maurice Dufrène. *From* Modern French Decorative Art *by Léon Deshairs*

## CHAIRS

Armchairs are low and heavy with carved backs and sloping arms. All are heavily padded and upholstered. Legs are short ending in straight stump or ball feet. The armchairs of this type are U or ⊔- shaped, and usually the wooden frame is visible only around the base, although some armchairs have a complete outside framework

Armchair and side chair of carved wood. Sue et Mare, circa 1920–1925. *From Modern French Decorative Art by Léon Deshairs*

of wood with modernistic inlay patterns of squares or triangles. Other chairs are barrel or gondola shaped with heavy circular bases. Sometimes, instead of arms, the chair has a back that plunges in a diagonal line and joins the wooden base. A smaller type of armchair has tall tapering legs. The backs of these chairs are oval, square or octagonal. This type of armchair and similar side chairs were used in the dining room. Some side chairs, by traditional designers such as Maurice Dufrène and Sue et Mare, are of carved wood in flowing lines suggesting drapery and the designs of the Louis Philippe period. The chairs of radical designers like Pierre Chareau, René Herbst and Djo-bourgeois often have frames of metal or chrome tubing and leather back, arm, and seat cushions.

*Top and bottom:* Tapestry sofas. G. L. Jaulmes. *From* Modern French Decorative Art *by Léon Deshairs*

## SOFAS

The sofas of the period also varied with the designer. Traditional sofas by such decorators as Maurice Dufrène or Sue et Mare were made to match the curved lines of the chairs. The sofas of the radical designers were heavy and often made to fit a particular wall space, such as an alcove, or else built in as a part of the architecture. End tables or shelves were often attached to the sofa.

## TABLES

Long rectangular tables have closed end supports with a heavy connecting stretcher resting on the floor. A dining table of burled walnut by Ruhlmann, which was exhibited in the 1925 Paris Exposition, has heavy U-shaped end supports. Other dining tables have heavy, square, circular or oval center supports and marble or glass tops. Small occasional tables were circular or square and usually were made with several tiered shelves. They have square or circular pedestals that rest directly on the floor. Similar tables were made with glass shelves and metal tubing legs. Some column tables were made with small cabinets and open shelves for books.

## CABINETS

The cabinet, or commode, is traditionally the most important article of French furniture and certainly this was true of cabinets of the 1920s and 1930s. They were large imposing pieces. The front is usually divided into doors and open shelves or spaces for books or bric-a-brac, such as pieces of art glass, pottery or sculpture. Cabinets often extend the complete length of a wall. A cabinet exhibited by Ruhlmann in 1927 has open shelves at each end for books and a center space with doors. A cabinet by Dominique called "Meuble de Collectionneur" has an open space in the center, which holds a large vase. Other cabinets hold pieces of bronze sculpture. Cabinets usually have marble tops and bronze or ivory plaques and handles.

## DESKS

A lady's writing desk in the Musée des Arts Décoratifs is of parchment, green lacquered wood and metal. The drawers are stepped in Art Deco style. Men's desks are usually flat topped with tiers of drawers within the side supports. Some are asymmetrical with drawers and shelves on one side. They are constructed of wood and metal. Similar desks of smaller proportions were made for women.

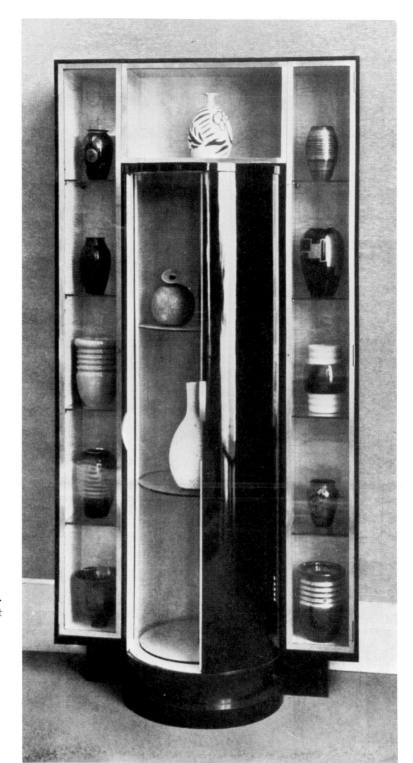

Cabinet for ceramics.
Léon Bouchet. *From* Art
et Décoration, *1930*

Lady's writing desk with ivory inlay. René Joubert and Philippe Petit, 1925 Paris Exposition. *Lent by the Galleries, Cranbrook Academy of Art, for the Finch College Museum Art Deco Exhibition*

Lady's writing table. Louis Sognot, 1925/26. *From* Modern French Decorative Art, *by Léon Deshairs*

## BEDS

Beds were heavy, broad and low. The head and foot boards were usually of wood, and the bed was often set on a low platform.

Many French designers were employed to decorate the *Ile-de France*, which was launched in 1927. Those whose work is shown include Ruhlmann, Martine, Sue et Mare, Etienne Kohlmann, Pierre Patout, Raymond Subes, Lalique and many others.

Although the Germans and Austrians were not invited to exhibit in the 1925 Exposition the French were aware of the work of Bruno Paul in Berlin and of Josef Hoffmann, Dagobert Peche and Koloman Moser of the Wiener Werkstätte through an exhibition held in Paris in 1910. Also, the work of the Bauhaus was known, and it influenced such avant-garde furniture designers as Le Corbusier, Charlotte Perriand, René Herbst, Robert Mallet-Stevens and Francis Jourdain, the famous silversmith Puiforcat and the jewelry designer Raymond Templier. Although the prejudice against the Germans continued for some years, the French designers must have known what was going on in Germany, since as mentioned previously, such magazines as *Deutsche Kunst und Dekoration* continued to publish, throughout the First World War. However, little was written in English then or now, and the work of the German craftsmen-designers has been comparatively ignored except in their own country.

Wood and gold leaf mirror. Dagobert Peche, Wiener Werkstätte, circa 1925. *From* Dagobert Peche *by Max Eisler*

Cabinet of amboyna with heavy fluting, vertical ivory stringing. Emile-Jacques Ruhlmann, circa 1931. Bronze doré plaque by S. Fourcault. *Deloranzo Gallery*

Cabinet. Bruno Paul, Berlin.
*From* Deutsche Kunst und
Dekoration, 1922/23

The architect–furniture designer Bruno Paul was the best-known designer of German furniture. Other important German furniture designers included Fritz August Breuhaus of Darmstadt, Karl Bertsch, Paul Griesser, Fritz Gross, Willi Foltin and Heinrich Straumer. German furniture displays more definite Art Deco angular characteristics than does French or English furniture. The forms are heavy, and dark woods are preferred. Many pieces are built up of stepped forms. The favorite decorative process of Josef Hoffmann was carving, and some pieces such as cabinets have carved flower rosettes in an allover geometric framework. One cabinet is ornately carved with grapevines on a trellis. Other pieces have zigzag borders and heavy fluting. Dining chairs have openwork X-patterns in their backs. X-shaped, carpenter's-workbench legs were often used on chairs and cabinets.

Cabinet with intarsia decoration. Victor Lurje, Vienna. *From* Deutsche Kunst und Dekoration, 1922/23

Mirror of silvered bronze and glass.
G. T. Rietveld, 1925. *Lent by Lillian
Nassau, Ltd., for the Finch College
Museum Art Deco Exhibition*

Armchairs are heavily upholstered with one continuous curve making
up the back and arms. Breuhaus decorated cabinets with carved
designs of deer and leaves on an allover fretwork of zigzags and
sharply curved angles. Later many surfaces were veneered with contrasting grains and wood colors. Intarsia and inlay were also important
methods of decoration, and complete scenes with figures and landscape are seen on important cabinets by such designers as Fritz Gross
and Willi Foltin.

When North German Lloyd's *Bremen* was built in 1928/29, Bruno
Paul, Fritz August Breuhaus, Alexander Schröder and other important
German decorators and designers of the period were commissioned
to do the decorations.

Art Deco was slow in being accepted in America, although by 1928
several exhibitions of French decorative art were sponsored by Lord &
Taylor and B. Altman. In 1928 the Metropolitan Museum gave space
to the R. H. Macy-sponsored "International Exhibition of Art in
Industry." The foremost designers and craftsmen of Europe were
invited to create rooms. The work of such well-known architects and
designers as Josef Hoffmann of Vienna, Bruno Paul of Berlin, Leleu of

Paris and Gio Ponti of Milan, Italy, was shown. Among the American designers were Kem Weber of Hollywood, Eugen Schoen, and William Lescaze. Other American interior designers of the period included Joseph Urban, Paul T. Frankl, Donald Deskey, Walter Dorwin Teague and Edward Aschermann.

Frank Lloyd Wright and Eliel Saarinen were the real innovators of the geometric approach to furniture design in America. Wright designed furniture for the houses that he built; the other architectural designers were employed for the most part in office decoration. The well-known women decorators of the period, Elsie de Wolfe, Rose Cumming, Marian Hall and Elsie Cobb Wilson, were busy producing period rooms with authentic antique furniture.

Round dining table with wood inlay. Eliel Saarinen, circa 1928. *Lent by the Galleries, Cranbrook Academy of Art, for the Finch College Museum Art Deco Exhibition*

Chair designed for Imperial Hotel, Tokyo.
Frank Lloyd Wright, circa 1920. *Lent by
Cooper-Hewitt Museum of Design for the
Finch College Museum Art Deco Exhibition*

In 1932 Radio City Music Hall was built as a part of Rockefeller
Center in New York City. From its architectural detail, its bronze
doors and plaques, to the decoration of its glamorous lobby, Radio
City Music Hall is the definitive expression of Art Deco in America.
The exterior is ornamented with colored plaques by Hildreth Meire,
and a series of bronze plaques over the main entrance doors illustrate
vaudeville acts from various countries by René Chambellan. The bronze
doors in the great entrance lobby are composed of panels, which are
also designed by René Chambellan.

The interior decoration of Radio City was under the direction of
Donald Deskey, who designed the furniture, lamps, fabrics and wall-

Act from vaudeville, Rockettes. Metal plaque by René Chambellan, 1932 Radio City Music Hall. Avenue of the Americas entrance. *Photograph John La Barca*

Act from vaudeville, German. Metal plaque by René Chambellan, 1932. Radio City Music Hall. Avenue of the Americas entrance. *Photograph John La Barca*

Act from vaudeville, Jewish. Metal plaque by René Chambellan, 1932. Radio City Music Hall. Avenue of the Americas entrance. *Photograph John La Barca*

Egyptian dancer. Bronze plaque from doors into auditorium by René Chambellan, 1932. Radio City Music
Hall. *Photograph John La Barca*

Grecian dancers. Bronze plaque from doors into auditorium by René Chambellan, 1932. Radio City Music
Hall. *Photograph John La Barca*

Masked dancers. Bronze plaque from doors into auditorium
by René Chambellan, 1932. Radio City Music Hall. *Photograph John La Barca*

Aluminum and painted wood side table. Donald Deskey, 1932. Radio City Music Hall. *Photograph Leland A. Cook*

papers. The rug in the lobby with its late Art Deco angular design was by Ruth Reeves, and a large sculpture figure on the mezzanine is by William Zorach a well-known American sculptor. The large mural above the stairway in the lobby is by Ezra Winter, and other murals on the mezzanine and in the various lounges are by Louis Bouché and Henry Billings.

Bench with aluminum base. Donald Deskey, 1932. Radio City Music Hall. *Photograph Leland A. Cook*

Wood cabinet, aluminum bands with marble top on which rest Sèvres vases presented to Radio City Music Hall Rockettes, 1937. Band around base of vases depicts the Rockettes. *Photograph Leland A. Cook*

Women's lounge at Radio City Music Hall. Small makeup tables of heavy glass attached to mirrors. Vertical light spandrels of frosted glass. Tan and brown plaid tapestry on walls. Animal mural by Henry Billings. Donald Deskey design. *Courtesy Radio City Music Hall*

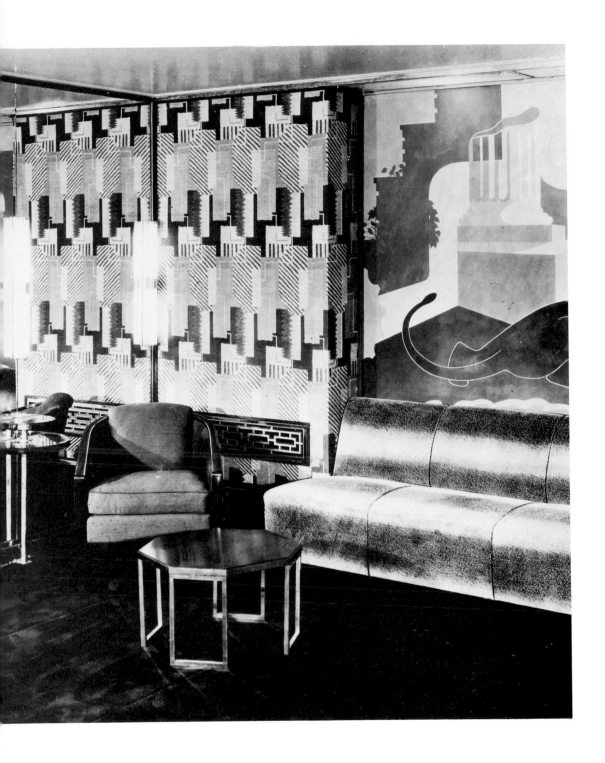

The smoking room at Radio City Music Hall. Aluminum paper with saga of tobacco blocked in deep tobacco brown. Donald Deskey design. *Courtesy Radio City Music Hall*

Main lobby, Radio City Music Hall, Rockefeller Center, New York City.
Interior decoration, Donald Deskey. Mural by Ezra Winter.

Sir Ambrose Heal and Sir Gordon Russell were the best-known British designers of furniture in the 1920s and 1930s. Russell's furniture tended toward the traditional and was influenced by country styles whereas that of Heal was more receptive to modern influences from Europe. The furniture of both were of straight-line construction. Veneer and line inlay were the popular methods of decoration, although Heal made some furniture painted black and decorated in bright orange, blue, green and white after the manner of the English Arts and Crafts Movement in the late nineteenth century. Peter Waals, R. W. Symonds, Robert Lutyens and Serge Chermayeff were among other English furniture designers of the era. The furniture of J. Dugald Stark was custom made for Stark Bros., it is distinguished by decorative grained veneering and also by the use of marquetry. Peter Waals's furniture was also custom made, and one ebony cabinet by Waals has painted decoration by Louise Powell. She and Alfred Powell also combined their designs on other furniture.

Tallboy of walnut veneered on mahogany with centers of English cherry, and turned feet of lignum vitae. J. Dugald Stark design. London, circa 1928. *From the* Studio Yearbook of Decorative Art, *1928*

## WROUGHT IRON AND METAL FURNITURE

Metal played an important part in both the architecture and the interior furnishings of the Art Deco period. Iron, copper and brass were sometimes combined in doors, stair railings, radiator covers, brackets and furniture. New beauty and possibilities of design and workmanship were discovered by the French craftsmen. Various metals were welded together to get new combinations of color and texture, and great importance was placed on design and workmanship.

Two types of motifs are present in the design of Art Deco ironwork. First, there are floral and animal designs, which, through their extensive use in the Exposition des Arts Décoratifs in 1925, became known to the world as Art Moderne motifs. The rounded conventionalized flowers and slender elongated animals were the most frequent motifs used in the 1920s. However, simple geometric patterns gradually came into favor, and simple lines, curves and angles more in harmony with the radical trend of furniture were seen in the decorative salons of 1928 and 1929.

Edgar Brandt was the most famous ironworker in the 1920s, and his gates, screens and decorative panels include a repertoire of characteristic Art Deco motifs. *The Oasis,* the famous five-fold screen at the 1925 Paris Exposition had a center panel of a fountain with stylized jets of water surrounded by geometric flowers and large leaves. Other screens by Brandt had leaping gazelles, baskets of fruit, vases or dancing nudes against a background of spirals. One of Brandt's famous decorative panels, *Les Cigognes* has an octagonal center panel of birds within a framework of rays and cloudlike spirals. Brandt also made decorative use of hammer marks. In the late 1920s Edgar Brandt showed a gradual breaking away from his naturalistic and conventional patterns and a strong tendency toward geometrical design. Instead of roses and rounded leaves, later designs were of joined crosses and diamond shapes.

Although Brandt was the most important ironworker, Raymond Subes was also well known. In his manner of working, Subes was also a traditionalist. He never lost sight of the demands and limitations of his craft. Even his most elaborate designs were made with a knowledge of the construction and with care for the utility, as well as the beauty of the object, whether it were a door, a radiator or a lamp base. Both Subes and Brandt made railings, panels and other pieces of iron-

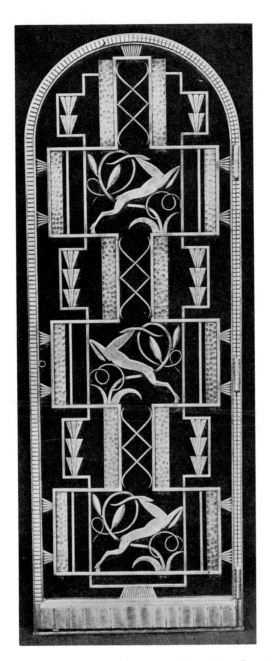

Wrought iron interior doorway. Edgar Brandt, circa
1925/26. *From* Modern French Decoration *by
Katharine Morrison Kahle (McClinton), 1930*

(a) wrought iron console and mirror, (b) wrought iron console, both by Edgar Brandt. *From* La Ferronnerie Moderne (Series 4), *by Henri Clouzot*

a

Wrought iron fire screen. Design of stylized fountain, flowers and leaves. Signed Edgar Brandt, 1924. *The Metropolitan Museum of Art*

b

work for the *Ile-de-France* in 1927. Other excellent ironsmiths were Paul Kiss, Gilbert Poillerat, Edward Schenck, Berge, Baguès Frères, Charles Piguet and Nics Frères.

Many pieces of furniture in the 1920s and 1930s were made of wrought iron and were quite ornate. At the beginning such decorative pieces as console tables and screens were the only articles made. These occasional pieces by Edgar Brandt and Raymond Subes were admired more as works of art than as pieces of furniture. Console tables are usually of graceful design, beautiful in ornamental detail, and topped with a slab of colored marble. There were also many small tables of wrought iron with marble tops. Round tables were made with tripod supports resting upon a marble base. Long dining tables were also made with wrought iron supports and marble or glass tops.

Lacquer screen doors. Dark green background framed in black, a design of angel and rocks in tones of gold. Wings of angel inlaid with eggshell, headdress with mother-of-pearl. Designed by Seraphin Soudbinin, executed by Jean Dunand, 1925/26. *Cooper-Hewitt Museum of Design, Smithsonian Institution*

Wrought iron console of vase design with marble top
and heavy hammer marks. *Nics Frères*

Two wrought iron occasional tables with scroll and leaf designs and marble tops. *Nics Frères*

Fire screen with scrolls and leaves. Gilbert Poillerat. *From* La Feronnerie Moderne *(Series 4)*, *by Henri Clouzot*

Fireplace equipment was another branch of wrought iron work. There were fire screens, firebacks and andirons. Poillerat made a great many andirons. Some were of simple wrought spiral designs, and others were of snakes, mermaids, jazz musicians and elongated dachshunds. Poillerat also made lamp bases of wrought iron in both conventionalized floral designs and in geometric patterns. In the late 1920s and 1930s, when furniture became more and more influenced by Cubism, metalwork designs also became more geometric, and zigzags, squares and triangles took the place of the earlier motifs.

The 1920s also saw the revival of the art of the locksmith. Door handles, doorplates, knockers and keys were all designed to harmonize with the furniture and other decorative elements. Many of the important designers including Puiforcat, Ruhlmann, Maurice Dufrène, Sue and Dominique made designs for architectural as well as furniture hardware. The designs for doorplates were usually simple line designs. However, occasionally there were sets such as the door plates and knobs called "Les Quatre Saisons," by Pierre Poisson. The designs consisted of nudes and flowers set in circles symbolical of the seasons— a basket of flowers for spring, a fish design for summer, geese for autumn and fire for winter.

a

Wrought iron andirons. (a) stylized
mermaids; (b) jazz musicians; (c)
Art Deco stepped design. Gilbert
Poillerat. *From* Art et Décoration,
*1930*

b

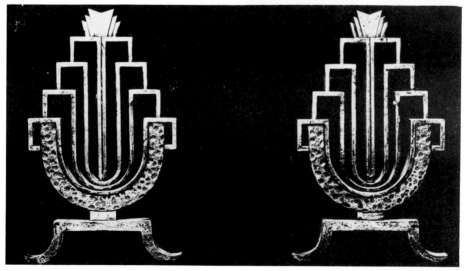

c

It was tubular furniture rather than wrought iron furniture that was to gain popularity in the next decade. The first tubular metal chair was made by Marcel Breuer, in 1925, when he was director of the Bauhaus furniture shops. Although the group of radical French furniture designers, including Pierre Chareau and Djo-bourgeois, were experimenting with tubular metal at this time, there was no metal furniture in the rooms at the 1925 Paris Exposition. However, there was an increasing acceptance of metal furniture and by 1927, Thonet was manufacturing metal furniture in Germany after designs by Le Corbusier, Mies van der Röhe and Marcel Breuer. In the 1927 Salon des Artistes Décoratifs, however, the only tubular furniture exhibited was occasional smoking and lamp tables, which consisted of glass shelves around an aluminum tube set on a circular aluminum base. These were shown in interiors by J. J. Adnet and Maurice Matet.

The most effective use of metal was in combination with thick plate glass meant to sit on tables and dressing tables. Tubular metal furniture gradually became acceptable for bars and smoking rooms, and Robert Mallet-Stevens designed chrome-plated metal and painted metal tubing office furniture. Le Corbusier, Jeannert, and Perriand designed chairs of metal tubing with large leather cushions, but it was 1930 before metal furniture was popularly accepted by the general public.

Armchair of metal tubing and wicker. Mies van der Rohe, 1927, for Thonet, Germany

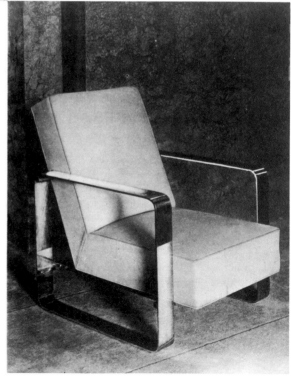

Two armchairs: *above,* with metal tubing and
upholstered seat; *right,* with metal frame and
upholstered back and seat. J. J. Adnet. *From*
Art et Décoration, *1930*

# 4 RUGS AND TEXTILES

When furniture began to take on modern functional forms and use materials such as plywood, glass and metal, it was obvious that the adaptations of old designs for upholstery, drapery and rugs were no longer harmonious. Fabrics with bolder patterns and better-wearing qualities were necessary not only for harmony of decoration but to meet the demands of a new informal age. To remedy this, some of the French ensembliers designed their own textiles for use in their interiors. Ruhlmann, Maurice Dufrène, Paul Follot, and Martine as well, designed their own fabrics.

However, the manufacturers of fabrics were alert to the change and were themselves searching for new designs, colors and weaving techniques to produce new textures. At first the designs employed motifs such as swags of flowers, urns, doves, fountains and strings of pearls, in an elegant but unmistakably twentieth-century style. The use of these traditional elements of design is particularly noticeable in the materials used by Emile-Jacques Ruhlmann and Paul Follot. The influence of the Ballets Russes brought about the popularity of bold color and Oriental imagery, and the craze for things Oriental led to the use of gold and silver metallic threads and the sheen of artificial silk. The designers Seguy and Edouard Bénédictus specialized in designs that were inspired by Eastern and African sources. In 1920, the album *Samarkande* illustrated the Oriental styles.

Seguy's album *Papillon* contained color sketches of various species of butterflies together with pages of butterfly designs. One design of green and black butterflies arranged on a stem has a bright orange ground. Another design is of green, black and yellow butterflies against an electric blue ground. Still another design is definitely Art Deco with repeats of orange, brown and black dots.

During the twenties, *Variations, Nouvelles Variations* and *Relais* albums contained designs made by Bénédictus for Brunet, Meunie et Cie. The *Variations* album, circa 1926, contained conventional flower designs in bold Ballets Russes colors, which may have been the inspiration for some of the floral designs used by Martine. There are also plates of geometric cubist designs.

Other fabric designers included Robert Bonfils and the painter Raoul Dufy, who worked for Bianchini-Férier, manufacturers of printed fabrics. Dufy, the best-known designer, began with prints blocked by hand from hand-cut blocks. His designs included flowers, agricultural scenes such as Les Moissonneurs, fishing scenes, La Jungle, Fruits d'Europe, Grand Feuillages and Les Anémones, all dating before 1930. Before that Dufy had designed large flower and leaf patterns with bold splashy color for Paul Poiret's Martine. Dufy also designed tapestries that were woven by the Beauvais factory. Suzanne Lalique, Stephany, Robert Mahias, André Drésa and Paul Véra also designed fabrics with garlands and urns of flowers in the Art Deco manner before the influence of Cubism. The Japanese painter Foujita and André Mare and Louis Sue also designed fabrics.

Elise Djo-bourgeois designed fabrics and carpets in geometrical patterns of gray with red, green or yellow for the interiors created by her husband. Madame Sonia Delaunay also created patterns of angular squares, rectangles, triangles and stripes. Her designs in bold primary colors were made for costumes and dress accessories. In 1928 an exhibition of Toile Imprimée et Papier Peint at Musée Galliera, Raoul Dufy, Mlle Suzanne Guiguichon, of Galeries Lafayette, Adrien Garcelon of A la Place Clichy, René Herbst, Martine and others exhibited new designs in both traditional and Cubist patterns.

Designs for silk fabrics. *Top left:* fern fronds, Coudyser for Lauer. *Top right:* damask with bouquets, ribbons and baskets of fruit, E. Kohlmann for Studium-Louvre. *Bottom:* Raoul Dufy for Bianchini, Férier. *From Modern French Decorative Art by Léon Deshairs*

Printed silk. Designed by Foujita for Lesur, circa 1925

Lucien Bouix exhibited printed cottons in designs composed of circles, lines and angles in striking blues, magentas, greens and blacks. Materials exhibited by Brunet, Meunie et Cie also showed an influence of Cubist designs, which were suitable with the bold metal furniture. In the same exhibition Maurice Dufrène showed rich printed silk velours, and Ruhlmann and Louis Sue exhibited silks with traditional motifs of vases, jets of water and swags in French elegance. The designs of Paul Dumas also harked to tradition rather than Cubism.

One of the foremost producers of modern fabrics was Rodier. The textures and motifs of his materials were inspired by the native arts of Africa and although some designs included bold leaves and flowers the majority of them were geometric. The French decorator often used the same fabric for draperies, furniture upholstery, and sometimes one wall of the room was covered with the fabric or with a matching wallpaper. The same artists who designed wallpapers also designed textiles. In the exhibition of printed textiles and wallpapers at the Musée Galliera in 1928, wallpapers by Bénédictus, Jacques Camus, Stephany, Mlle Anne Marie Fontaine for Galeries Lafayette, Mlle Suzanne Fontan, Mlle Colette Gueden for Au Printemps, René Gabriel for Les Papiers Peints de France, Paul Follot for A la Place Clichy; Marie Laurencin, André Groult, Fressinet, and others were on display. The Société Française des Papiers Peints exhibited papers designed by Stephany, Ruhlmann, Sue et Mare and Mlle Suzanne Fontan. Among the designs were Papillons, Magnolia, Bouquet, La Rose Moderne, Les Oiseaux, Animaux and line and angle abstractions. There were also characteristic colorful papers by Martine with names that suggest their design—Les Eucalyptus, Les Jacinthes, Les Pavots and Les Roses Jaunes. All were in bold floral patterns of purples, lavenders, blues, pinks and greens.

Art Deco rugs and tapestries followed the designs popular for draperies and upholstery materials. At first the designs consisted of decorative floral fantasies, trelliswork, arabesques, medallions and baskets and garlands of conventionalized flowers that echoed earlier traditional designs but were combined with the brilliant color inspired by the Ballets Russes. The rugs and draperies of Martine were a mass of brilliant roses and other conventionalized flowers on dark backgrounds. Similar floral rugs were designed by Paul Follot, Maurice Dufrène, André Groult and Sue et Mare. But the trend toward geometrical designs and modernism gradually became more important, and after 1926 the influence of Cubism and African design is dominant. Da Silva Bruhns brought in a new barbaric influence with his geometric patterns in reds, browns and blacks woven in heavy hand-tufted wool. Cubist designs for carpets were also made by Robert Mallet-Stevens, Jacques Doucet, Fernand Léger and Stephany. Rug designs by Joubert et Petit for Décoration Intérieure Moderne (DIM)

Pink, rose and brown wall-paper on gold field. Garden scene with trellis and fountain. France, 1920. *Cooper-Hewitt Museum of Design, Smithsonian Institution*

Rug with geometric design. Da Silva Bruhns, circa
1927. *From* Modern French Decoration *by Katharine
Morrison Kahle (McClinton)*

Rug with cubist design. Da Silva Bruhns, 1928. *From* Modern French Decoration *by Katharine Morrison Kahle (McClinton)*

included patterns with such names as Tropique, Samoa, Islam, Circles, La Nuit and Dame de Coeur. The names indicate the variety of the designs. In 1929, rug designs by the decorators DIM covered such subjects as the circus, music, tennis, pipes, ships, bridges and "La Chasse," all telling a story in a fascinating cubistic manner.

There was also revival of tapestry design. Manzana-Pissarro, the son of the painter Pissarro, set up a workshop at Aubusson, and Gustave Jaulmes and his wife in their workshop at Neuilly had considerable influence on the tapestry revival. A tapestry, La Nativité, was exhibited in the exhibition "Les Années '25" in 1966.

Such designers as Charles Dufresne, Robert Bonfils and Gustave Jaulmes made cartoons for Gobelins tapestries. Their subjects were taken from contemporary life. Jaulmes as well as Raoul Dufy and Paul Véra also made tapestry designs for Beauvais, and various other artists designed for the Aubusson factory. Other small independent workshops also produced tapestries from designs by Léger, Picasso, Paul Véra, Max Vibert and Jean Lurçat. Such motifs as the airplane, motors and tennis were used on the tapestries titled Outdoor Sports, Modern Dance, or Buses in the Forest; similar patterns were made for upholstery. Though few rugs or upholstery materials remain for the collector, there are modern tapestries available, although the prices are necessarily high.

In Germany the weaving workshop of the Bauhaus produced wall hangings, rugs and tapestries by such painter-weavers as Hedwig Jungnick, Benita Otte, Paul Klee, and especially Gunta Stolzl.

From 1926 to 1932 Gunta Stolzl directed the weaving at the Dessau Bauhaus, which also produced designs by Anni Albers, Otti Berger and Liz Beyer.

In Holland, the paintings of Piet Mondrian of Theo van Doesburg, both artists connected with de Stijl, had an influence on the design of rugs and tapestries.

Modern rugs and drapery and upholstery materials had little popularity in England in the 1920s; most houses were furnished with antique furniture and thus called for traditional designs. Searching through the volumes of the *Studio Yearbook of Decorative Art* one sees very little evidence of modernist design. However, the firm of W. Foxton, Ltd. was known for its printed cottons and tablecloths in modern floral and geometric designs by such designers as Gladys Barraclough and Minnie McLeish. Sefton & Co. printed textiles by the

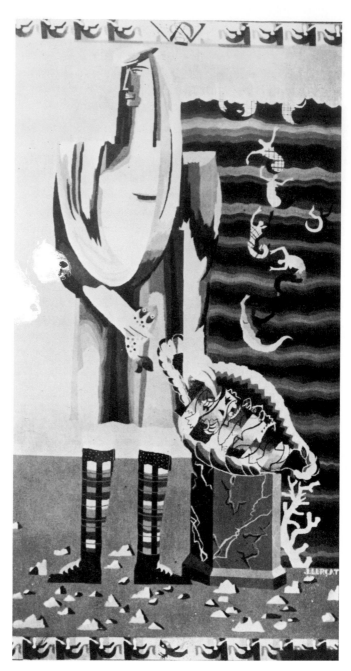

Tapestry by Jean Lurçat. *From* Art et Décoration, *1929*

designers George Sheringham and Harry Clarke. They also printed silk handkerchiefs in modern patterns. There was also a group of designers who made hand-printed textiles around 1928. These included Dorothy Larcher and Phyllis Barron. Their designs were based on abstract geometrical repeats. Other modern English designers included Paul Nash, E. McKnight Kauffer and Marion Dorn. Marion Dorn is known especially for her work as a designer of rugs with bold geometrical motifs. In the 1930s some of her designs were made by Wilton carpets. Rancati and Eric Bagge designed rugs for Waring & Gillow.

Design in American textiles was directed toward patterns that would be harmonious with period furniture styles, and modernist motifs were not popular until the late twenties. In 1927 R. H. Macy sponsored the International Exhibition of Art in Industry, and in 1928 Lord & Taylor sponsored an exhibition of French Decorative Art; the same year the Grand Rapids Market Association featured Art Moderne in its summer exhibition. These shows brought Art Deco to the attention of the designers in America, and the Chicago Century of Progress in 1933 displayed furniture and decorative art in harmony with the modern architecture of the exposition. Ruth Reeves was a well-known designer of fabrics and rugs of this time. Other modern American artists who designed for textile manufacturers included Henriette Reiss who designed rugs for Bigelow and for Ralph H. Pearson; Thomas H. Benton also designed hand-hooked rugs for Ralph H. Pearson. Teresa Kilham designed for R. H. Macy. Donald Deskey produced rug designs for the New England Guild, while Walter Dorwin Teague designed for Marshall Field & Co. in the 1930s. Ilonka Karasz, Winold Reiss and the photographer Edward Steichen designed fabrics in the late 1920s. In 1925 Steichen made designs of boxes, matches and lumps of sugar for silks manufactured by the Stehli Silk Corporation. Interesting designs were made for rugs and fabrics based on the theory of mathematics as explained in *The Mathematical Basis of the Arts* by Joseph Schillinger.

Designs for lace and embroidery in Art Deco patterns were made by Dagobert Peche and other designers of the Wiener Werkstätte and also by women in the various German workshops. Expressionist embroideries on cushions in bold angular designs by Frau von Alesch were illustrated in *The Studio* in 1927. Such embroideries were also

Silkscreen print on cotton,
using tans to reddish brown.
Ruth Reeves, circa 1930–1935.
*Cooper-Hewitt Museum of
Design, Smithsonian Institu-
tion*

Rose red, green and tan rug. Designed by Loja Saarinen, woven by Walborg
Nordquist, 1928. *The Galleries, Cranbrook Academy of Art*

made for tea cozies, table covers and ladies' bags. Lilli Vetter was known for her fine embroidered scenes of modern design; one, of leaping deer, is in the Art Deco manner. Fini Skarica of Vienna made embroidered doilies and tablecloths of cubistic design wth German inscriptions.

In France, modernistic tablecloths and doilies were designed and manufactured by Rodier. Unique abstract designs of shells, seaweed and fish were made in lace called point de Nice by Madame Chabert-Dupont. These tablecloths, table mats, curtains and wall hangings were made by hand in an original stitch that resembled the ironwork designs of Edgar Brandt.

In Italy, designers were active both in table linen and in finer embroideries such as on net and organdy.

Rug, blues and red. Designed by Joseph Schillinger according to his system as explained in *The Mathematical Basis of the Arts. Courtesy Mrs. Joseph Schillinger*

Lace. Dagobert Peche, Wiener Werkstätte, 1920. *From* Dagobert Peche *by Max Eisler*

a

b

(a) embroidered pillow, black on white, Gertrud Frenzel, Charlottenburg; (b) embroidered pillow, Emmy Zweybrück, Vienna. *From* Deutsche Kunst und Dekoration, *1918/ 19*

Embroidery on linen tablecloth. Italian. *Roberto Aloi,*
*L' Arredamento Moderno, 1939*

Embroidery on organdy. Contessina Pia di Valmarana, Venice. *Roberto Aloi, L'Arredamento Moderno, 1934*

Embroidered picture. Hedwig
Dülberg, Arnheim. *From*
Deutsche Kunst und Dekora-
tion, *1920*

Tablecloth. Josef Hoffmann, Wiener Werkstätte, 1905.

# 5 CLOCKS, LIGHTING FIXTURES AND LAMPS

CLOCKS ARE AN INTERESTING CATEGORY FOR ART DECO COLLECTORS. CLOCK cases of the 1920s and 1930s were made in all kinds of materials: glass, metal, porcelain, marble, wood, silver and gold. The decoration of clocks followed that of furniture and the other decorative arts of the period. In the early 1920s, the most popular clocks were of gilded bronze and marble and were ornamented with flowers and fruit in vases, in cornucopias or on trellises. Sometimes the designs included doves and nude or veiled figures. Clocks of this type were designed by Maurice Dufrène, Léon Jallot, M. Gauvenet, Gallerey, Paul Follot and other well-known French designers. Ironwork and marble were combined in the clocks made by ironworkers Edgar Brandt, Raymond Subes, Paul Kiss and others. Many noted sculptors, including Antoine Bourdelle, also designed clock cases.

An exhibition of modern clocks at Musée Galliera in 1921 included clocks of various materials that were designed by important designers of the period. The designs represented both traditional and radical trends. Some were the work of ensembliers such as Selmersheim, others were by the makers. A clock with silhouettes of carved wood

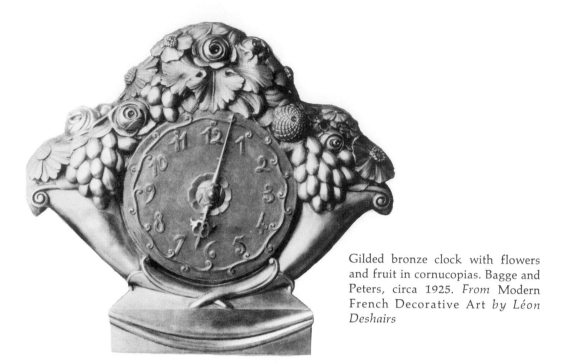

Gilded bronze clock with flowers and fruit in cornucopias. Bagge and Peters, circa 1925. *From* Modern French Decorative Art *by Léon Deshairs*

Marble clock with wrought iron for the lines of Egyptian headdress. Raymond Subes, circa 1927. *From* Modern French Decorative Art *by Léon Deshairs*

Marble clock on carved and gilt wood base.
Tony Selmersheim, exhibited Musée Galliera,
1921. *From* Art et Décoration, *1921*

was exhibited by de Bardyère. Raymond Subes made a clock case of
marble and forged iron; Capon Frères, a clock of hammered and engraved silver. A clock of crystal and enamel designed by Marcel
Goupy for the dealer Géo Rouard was one of the novelties of the
exhibition. Jean Dunand exhibited a clock case encrusted with gold
and silver lacquer. Other designers who exhibited clocks included
Szabo, Gallerey, and Paul Brindeau.

Hideous angular marble clocks with bronze mountings of cheap
design were made for popular consumption. These were often topped
with bronze figures of dancing girls, nudes or animals by such second-
rate bronze workers as Fritz Preiss. Mantelpiece garniture included
heavy marble clocks with bronze figures of Cleopatra, an Amazon, a
leopard with a pair of matching side figures or a pair of candelabra.
There were also glass, chrome and other metal clocks upheld by
psuedo-bronze nudes. These are all popular with collectors today.

Chrome clock held by nude figure. American, circa 1930. *Barry and Audrey Friedman, The Antiques Center of America*

Glass clock upheld by two pseudo-bronze nudes. Frankart, 1929. *From* The Jewelers' Circular, *July 18, 1929*

Glass clocks by Lalique were decorated with nude figures, flowers, ferns and other leaf designs, birds and butterflies. These designs were engraved on the glass. Often the clockface consisted of a round, square or dome-shaped slab of glass set on a marble or metal stand. Some clocks had sculptured figures of nudes or lovebirds. Other glassmakers including Daum, Sabino, André Hunebelle and Henri Navarre made similar clock cases. In the late 1920s Sabino and Hunebelle became important glassmakers. By 1930 Art Deco designs were changing due to the influence of Cubism, and clocks became more angular in form and decoration. The manufacturers of clockworks also changed the design and numbering on clockfaces, and bold numerals and Art Deco angular motifs decorated the metal faces of many clocks.

Glass clock with design of two parakeets. René Lalique, circa 1925. *Christie's*

Porcelain clock. M. Gauvenet, executed at Sèvres factory, 1925–1927. *From* The Studio Yearbook of Decorative Arts, *1927*

In the thirties clock designs became simpler. A silvered bronze clock signed by Albert Cheuret in 1930 has the sweeping lines of an Egyptian headdress. Clock cases of porcelain were made by Sèvres of Meissen porcelain and by lesser-known china manufacturers. Cheaper cases were made of pottery. Many of these were of poor design, and some clocks in this category can be classed as kitsch.

Art Deco clocks of wood with decorations of intarsia were made in Italy in the early 1930s. These had both round and square forms. Clocks were also made in striking cubes, and in circular and triangular shapes. A unique clock of dice design, which was an Art Deco fad, was of enamel with blue dots and a diamond-shaped face. The clock was made by J. E. Caldwell of Philadelphia in the 1930s.

Clocks with intarsia decoration. Italian.
*Roberto Aloi, L'Arredamento Moderno, 1934*

Clock of black lacquer, bronze, coral and
chalcedony. Cartier, circa 1925. *Lent by Jon
Nicholas Streep for the Finch College
Museum Art Deco Exhibition*

A large number of clocks were also made by Cartier and other
jewelers. These clocks were ornamented with gold and silver or
lacquered and decorated with ivory, amber and precious stones, such
as diamonds, rubies and emeralds. One Cartier clock made around
1926 has a case of transparent quartz topaz and gold and is set with
diamonds, coral and jade. The face is black enamel with mother-of-
pearl numerals. A small gold and jade boudoir clock was decorated
with black niello arabesques. It stands on carved coral and onyx
supports. A red and black enamel clock set on an onyx base is ornamented with rose diamonds, cabochon rubies and platinum. A clock
of black lacquer and bronze is set with coral and chalcedony. Another
elaborate small crystal clock mounted with enameled gold and rose
diamonds was made by Cartier around 1930. An important clock of
onyx, diamonds and mother-of-pearl has two jade lion figures that
stand on either side of the clockface. Another clock combines silver,
ivory, plastic and diamonds.

Dice clock, enamel with blue dots. J. E. Caldwell &
Co., circa 1930. *Lent by Lillian Nassau, Ltd., for the
Finch College Museum Art Deco Exhibition*

Clock of silver and ivory. Red,
black, and amber colored plastic,
and diamonds. Cartier, circa 1930.
*Parke-Bernet Sale, April 1970*

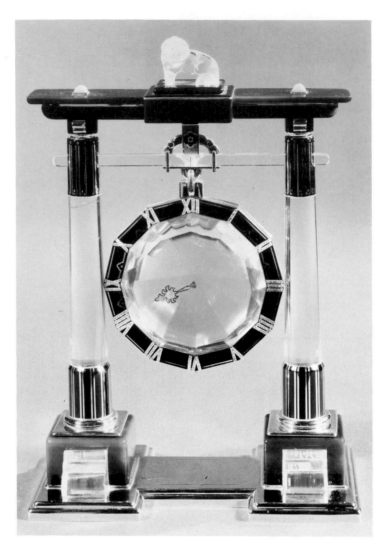

Crystal and enamel clock. Cartier, 1930. *Parke-Bernet Sale, January 30, 1969*

## LIGHTING FIXTURES AND LAMPS

Lighting fixtures and lamps have always followed the lead of decorative architectural and furniture styles. Thus, when a new style is born, its motifs, symbols, materials and structural characteristics are adapted to forms of lighting. Technical breakthroughs in the lighting industry after World War I transformed the ways in which lighting was used. In the past the fixture was the decoration whereas in modern lighting light itself produces decorative effects. Modern lighting employs and capitalizes on the materials of light production, metal and glass. Instead of trying to hide the globes, the globe itself is made into a fixture that not only diffuses the light but performs the aesthetic duty of creating patterns of light as design. The new lighting fixtures were in harmony with the decoration of the room and reflected the same modern spirit. The lighting fixtures were designed with simple lines, angles and juxtaposed squares, circles and triangles to form new harmonies and designs. Glass and metal were the important materials and they were used in clean-cut angular forms. The various types of fixtures—table or floor lamps, wall or ceiling fixtures—used these simple materials and followed this general design. The fixtures depend on form and contour for effect. Plain slabs of glass or simply etched geometrical designs are the decoration. The lamps and lighting fixtures of Lalique are an exception. They are decorated with elaborately etched floral or geometric designs.

For the general indirect lighting of a room, fixtures are often placed within the walls. Square or rectangular niches enclosed with frosted glass are placed horizontally or vertically to aid in the decorative balance of the room. Architecture also plays a part in the lighting scheme. Domes and ceilings act as reflectors, and the planes and coronas create patterns of bright light and dark shadows. Concealed light globes are placed in beveled cornices and columns. Slender tubes of neon lighting are placed in geometric patterns in walls and ceiling beams or set in square, triangular or rectangular boxes. Small wall lights are often set within the wall to produce a gay and festive effect of stars. Chandeliers were designed to suggest fountains and jets of water. Lalique designed glass chandeliers with motifs of starfish, jungle plants and animal forms. Angular slabs of frosted glass were assembled in other chandeliers. In *Mobilier et Décoration*, 1928, a

Ballroom in southern France with indirect lighting producing a starry effect.
*From* Modern French Decoration *by Katharine Morrison Kahle (McClinton)*

group of chandelier designs by Sabino drew inspiration from leaves and flowers. Graduating rows of conventional leaves or flower petals formed the stepped fixtures and give a diffused light with the source of the light itself concealed. Wrought iron wall brackets designed by Edgar Brandt were made to hold bowls of Lalique glass.

Wrought iron designs against a background of opaque glass or alabaster form the materials for many beautiful lamps. Lalique often combined his glass designs with the wrought iron standards of Edgar Brandt. Sometimes the iron standards are in the forms of conventionalized animals or plants, or they may be of geometric design.

a

Wrought iron lamps: (a) Gilbert Poillerat, (b) Nics Frères, circa 1929. *From* La Ferronnerie Moderne (*Series 4*), *by Henri Clouzot*

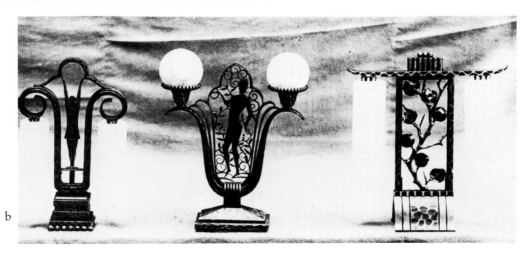

b

Wrought iron and glass hanging light fixture. 1930s.
*Lent by Lillian Nassau, Ltd., for the Finch College
Museum Art Deco Exhibition*

Bronze table lamp. Emile-
Jacques Ruhlmann, 1925. *Lent
by Lillian Nassau, Ltd., for
the Finch College Museum
Art Deco Exhibition*

Many hanging and floor lamps are a combination of glass and
wrought iron. Lamps were also made of glass bowls by Daum, Müller
Frères, and Sabino as well as Lalique and André Hunebelle. Ruhlmann
and others designed lamps to be used together with their furniture.
There were also lamps with pottery and porcelain as well as wood
bases. Some have shapes that graduate like a skyscraper and others
are round, rectangular, hexagonal or octagonal.

Glass lamp with geometric design. André Hunebelle. *From* Art et Décoration, *1931*

Carved crystal lamp on wooden base. Circa 1930. *Lent by Lillian Nassau, Ltd., for the Finch College Museum Art Deco Exhibition*

Lamp on a green glass base with silver metal mounting. Jean-Michel Frank, circa 1928. *Cooper-Hewitt Museum of Design, Smithsonian Institution*

Many lamp bases were made by well-known potters. Robert Lallemand made lamp bases of cubistic, stepped forms decorated with enameled cubistic designs in black and red and black and green. Matching parchment shades were made by Pierre Laville. Robj made an amusing piano lamp in the form of a cowboy. Bottles for lamps were also made by Mme Mina-Loy in the 1930s. The subjects included La Fontaine, Corne d'abondance, Femme cariatide, and Les trois amours. There were also figures of the Vendôme column, the Eiffel Tower and of Louis Philippe, Napoleon III, Gambetta and Carnot.

A popular type of lamp consisted of a ball or cylinder of frosted or etched glass held up by nude figures and set on a stepped base. The

Bronze and glass lamp on marble base. *Gladys Koch, The Antiques Center of America*

Bronze figures holding mosaic-covered light globe. Circa 1930. *George Schwartz, The Antiques Center of America*

best of these lamps were made of wrought iron or bronze, but there were many combinations of simulated bronze, chrome, pewter or plaster. In the mid- to late 1920s a New York company called Frankart manufactured many of these lamps with nude figures and gaudy glass globes of round, square or rectangular forms. These fixtures were stamped with the name "Frankart" and the patent date. Frankart also made a clock. They put out a handbook to illustrate their line of products for the season 1929/30.

One of the most interesting lighting developments of the Art Deco period was the illuminated plaque or figure. These popular decorative lighting pieces may have first been introduced by Lalique to display his glass to the best effect. Whatever may have prompted their making, the idea caught on, and illuminated plaques and glass figures with concealed light globes were made by all the manufacturers of decorative glass, including Sabino, le Verrier, Daum and Genet & Michon.

There were numerous standing lamps with wrought iron, bronze and other metal bases. Lalique and Edgar Brandt combined to produce attractive floor lamps, and in an exhibition in the late twenties, a huge copper snake held up a cone of Lalique glass.

*Clarité.* Nude figure of white metal on marble base holding glass ball light globe. *From* Catalogue, *by Max le Verrier, 1925, Vincent Primavera*

*Top and bottom:* Lamps with white metal nude figures. Frankart. *From* The Jewelers' Circular, *March 21, 1929. Hallmark Inc., Fifth Avenue*

*Offrande.* White metal figures on marble base holding bowl with floral design on glass dome concealing light globe. Signed Fayral. *From* Catalogue, *by Max le Verrier, 1925, Vincent Primavera*

Floor lamp with three cones flaring upward and a round base. *Kingswood School, Cranbrook, Michigan*

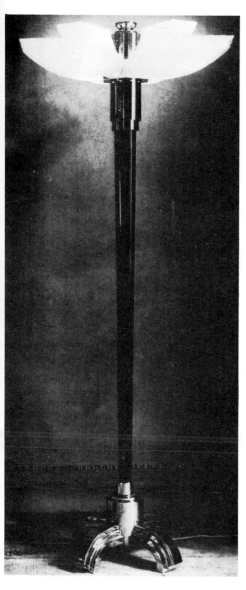

Metal standing lamp with
glass bowl. Edgar Brandt.
*From* La Ferronnerie Moderne
*(Series 4) by Henri Clouzot*

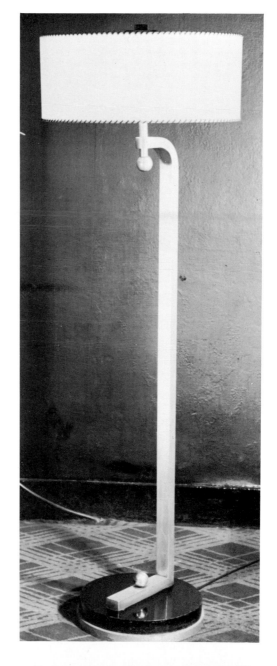

Aluminum and painted wood floor
lamp. Donald Deskey, for Radio
City Music Hall, 1932. *Photograph
by Leland A. Cook*

Standing lamp aluminum and painted wood in torch form. Donald Deskey
for Radio City Music Hall, 1932. *Photograph by Leland A. Cook*

# 6 POTTERY AND PORCELAIN

A DISTINCTION SHOULD BE MADE BETWEEN ART DECO POTTERY-CRAFTSMEN and the manufacturers of pottery and porcelain. Both types of ceramics were made in the various countries, and both types are available to collectors today. The pieces by artist-craftsmen are one of a kind, and since interest has turned to this type of pottery today the prices are keeping pace with the demand. The pottery and porcelain made by manufacturers are less expensive and more available since duplicates were made. This type of pottery often represents the kitsch phase of Art Deco and is found in many antique shops and thrift shops; the signed pieces by artist-craftsmen are often sold at auction or found only in better shops.

Of the many pottery-craftsmen working in France between 1910 and the 1930s Emile Decoeur, Emile Lenoble, Georges Serré, Henri Simmen, Jean Mayodon, and André Metthey were the best known. Decoeur made sandstone pottery and porcelain and applied the Art Deco motifs of roses, spirals and geometric decoration to both. His finest vases and bowls were made in the mid-1920s and are covered with blue, green, pink, yellow and white enamels, but little

Pottery vase. Emile Decoeur, circa 1925. *Lent by the Galleries, Cranbrook Academy of Art, for Finch College Museum Art Deco Exhibition*

Stoneware vase. Emile Lenoble, 1925. *Lent by the Galleries, Cranbrook Academy of Art, for the Finch College Museum Art Deco Exhibition*

other decoration. They are stamped on the base with the name or initials of the maker. Lenoble stoneware pottery is decorated with floral or geometric motifs, incised, modeled in low relief, or painted, sometimes under the glaze and sometimes over it. His pottery made on the wheel included vases, bowls and bottles that show the influence of Oriental wares. The pieces are stamped on the foot and base. Georges Serré produced heavy sandstone ware incised with simple geometric motifs. Henri Simmen made vases with crackle and sea-green glazes enriched with enamel. They are marked "H. Simmen." Jean Mayodon hand-modeled or painted figures and animals on his pottery. In the 1925 Paris Exposition, Mayodon exhibited a stemmed shallow bowl of red crackle glaze with gold luster and nude figures. The painter-engraver René Buthaud painted rounded outlined female figures in colored enamels on squat oval forms, some of which were made for the dealer Géo Rouard. The early pottery of André Metthey is sandstone. Later he made earthenware and employed the well-known painters Bonnard, Derain, Matisse, Redon, Rouault, Vuillard, Louis Valtat, E. Othon Friesz and Vlaminck to decorate the pieces. Vlaminck and Derain later made and decorated their own pottery as did Picasso.

Salt-glaze stoneware vase with speckled buff coloring with brown enriched with gold enamel. Signed "H. Simmen," circa 1925. *Sotheby & Co.*

Red crackle-glaze, shallow bowl on slender stem with gold luster and nude figures. Jean Mayodon, 1925 Paris Exposition. *Lent by the Galleries, Cranbrook Academy of Art, for the Finch College Museum Art Deco Exhibition*

Vase with brown nude figure. René Buthaud, 1925. *Lent by Lillian Nassau, Ltd., for the Finch College Museum Art Deco Exhibition*

Pottery vase with figures. René Buthaud, circa 1925. *Lent by the Galleries, Cranbrook Academy of Art, for the Finch College Museum Art Deco Exhibition*

Pottery vase. Jean Luce, circa 1929. *Lent by the Galleries, Cranbrook Academy of Art, for Finch College Museum Art Deco Exhibition*

The decorators Maurice Dufrène and Francis Jourdain also designed ceramics. Jourdain sold faience and glazed earthenware in his decorating shop. The decorating departments of Parisian department stores also designed and sold figures, animals and tableware made to harmonize with their interiors. These inexpensive vases and lamps were in popular Art Deco designs including large leaves and bold flowers, nude figures and birds. Some of these pieces were made for Primavera at Au Printemps, and were signed by Helène Gatelet and Madeleine Sougez. Pottery animals were made for them by Jean Jacques Adnet; pottery figures of nudes were made by Marcel Renard in the late 1920s, and Colette Gueden designed pottery figurines for Primavera in the 1930s. Ceramics with squared and stepped forms and gay painted figures in red and black were made by Robert Lallemand. Such manufacturers as Haviland, Sèvres and the dealer Géo Rouard employed modern artists to design their wares. Jean Dufy, the brother of Raoul Dufy, the painter, designed and decorated porcelain for

*Left:* ceramic figures of cubistic design in blue green. Zsolnay, 1930. *Center:* glass vase with black and silver geometric decoration. Czechoslovakia. *Right:* vase with Art Deco motifs—sun, clouds, checkerboard, and Eiffel Tower. Signed "Lallemand," circa 1927. *Frank Weston and Robert Morgan, The Antiques Center of America*

Haviland. The designs included a château with towers and a pattern of pink roses enhanced with gilt. The plate with the turreted château, which was exhibited at the 1925 Paris Exposition, is marked "Theodore Haviland," in green; "Theodore Haviland, Limoges, France," in red; "Exposition des A.D. Paris 1925," in blue; "TH" impressed and the signature of Jean Dufy in blue. Suzanne Lalique also designed and painted porcelain for Haviland. Plates, from around 1925, have grapevines and grapes in black, green and silver. They are marked with the usual green and red Haviland marks and the signature of Suzanne Lalique in blue. Haviland also manufactured five table services for Géo Rouard that were decorated by the designer Marcel Goupy. These included the following named patterns: Antibes, decorated in black rose and gold; Marquises, with stylized flowers and birds in polychrome decoration; Montjoie, decorated in black; Bombay, in green, ocher and gold; and Christine, in black. These services, together with four services decorated by Marcel Goupy and manufactured by Keramis, Belgique, were exhibited in the 1925 Paris Exposition and again in "Les Années '25" in the Musée des Arts Décoratifs in 1966.

Porcelain vase with blue and brown decoration. Sèvres, circa 1925. *Lent by Lillian Nassau Ltd., for the Finch College Museum Art Deco Exhibition*

The manufactory of Sèvres employed artists to design vases, fountains and table settings for their exhibit in the 1925 Exposition. The designers included the well-known artists Mme Lalique, Raoul Dufy, Ruhlmann, Nathan, Jaulmes, Serrière, Robert Bonfils and the brothers Martel. Sculptors who designed small porcelain figures for Sèvres included Poupelet, Pierre Poisson, Auguste Guénot, Fernand David, Pommier and Arnold.

Bing and Gröndahl of Copenhagen also produced work in the modern manner in the 1920s. Kay Nielsen and Jean Ganguin were the well-known designers of Danish porcelain at this period. Figures by Kay Nielsen were traditional in subject matter and included such mythological figures as Neptune, Venus and the Satyrs. Other figures in three-corner hats and fancy dress showed the influence of eighteenth-century porcelains. Many shapes were modern, and some of the designs tended toward Cubism. Both Bing & Gröndahl and the Royal Porcelain Manufactory exhibited at the 1925 Paris Exposition. The sandstone and porcelain animals of Kund Kyhn and the porcelain mounted in metal by P. Proschowski attracted special attention.

In Holland the best-known potters of the 1920s included Chr. Lanooy, Bert. Menhuis, Colenbrander, Hildo Krop, C. Van der Sluys and Lion-Cachet.

In 1903 Josef Hoffmann and Koloman Moser founded the Wiener Werkstätte in Vienna. Even the early work of Josef Hoffmann showed characteristics later seen in Art Deco. His distinctive black and white linear designs in squares and oblongs were used on porcelain vases and for table settings. Porcelain figures with black decoration were made by M. Powolny and B. Löffer as early as 1914, and the dancing pottery figures of Arnold Rönnebeck date from the early 1920s. Although the work of Hoffmann himself remained distinguished and dignified throughout his years with the Wiener Werkstätte, that of many other designers in the group took on the exotic and frivolous whimsies of Art Deco.

German ceramics of the 1920–30 period were influenced by the Bauhaus designers whose style was based on the cube, the rectangle and the circle. These Cubist tendencies are reflected in the shapes of teapots and coffeepots whose contours became angled or straight lined. This precision of line is seen in the ceramics produced by the Rosenthal factory in the 1920s and 1930s. Rosenthal also made porcelain vases and figures in Art Deco style, some in modern adaptations of Pierrot and Pierrette and other theatrical figures, and some in modern costume, such as the bather in contemporary black bathing suit, slippers and rubber bathing cap. Many of the figures have the signature of the artist as well as the Rosenthal factory stamp. Individual designers, such as Marianne Meyfarth of Cologne, decorated porcelain with gold and enamel, and many of the ceramic figures by the

Pair of vases with nude figures in landscape. Signed Tono Zoelch, for Rosenthal, circa 1931. *Carol Ferranti, The Antiques Center of America*

Porcelain figures. *Top left:* girl in Turkish costume. Signed D. Charol, for Rosenthal. *Center:* girl in black bathing suit, shoes and cap. Meier, Austria. *Right:* decorative figure, Austrian. All circa 1925–1930. *Fred Silberman, The Antiques Center of America*

Porcelain plate with blue and gold painted design. Marianne Meyfarth, Cologne. *From* Deutsche Kunst und Dekoration, *1928*

Ceramic figure. Vally Wieselthier, circa 1927. *From* Deutsche Kunst und Dekoration, *1927/28*

Porcelain covered dish with gold ornamentation. Richard Ginori, circa 1924. *Lent by Lillian Nassau Ltd., for Finch College Museum Art Deco Exhibition*

well-known Vally Wieselthier were of Art Deco subject matter. Max Läuger of Karlsruhe was noted for his glazed pottery bowls, vases and wall plaques. Läuger's pottery was handmade, and pieces are one of a kind.

In Italy, the Societé Richard-Ginori of Milan sold Art Deco faience and porcelain that was manufactured at San Cristoforo and Doccia. The two important designers of these wares were Gio Ponti and Saponaro. Designs included fluted bowls with figures of dancers and nautical scenes.

Boch pottery of Belgium has a gray crackled surface accented with bold contrasting bands of color or vivid Art Deco floral designs. Similar crackled pottery decorated with dancing figures and running deer was marked "Primavera Longiwy France." It was made for Atelier Primavera, Au Printemps, Paris.

Porcelain vases. *Bottom left:* Porcelaine de Doccia for Richard Ginori. *Bottom right:* Gio Ponti for Richard Ginori, circa 1925. *From* Art et Décoration

a

Two pottery vases. La Boch, Belgium, circa 1928. (a) *Lent by Stanley Insler, for the Finch College Museum Art Deco Exhibition.* (b) *Barry and Audrey Friedman*

b

Crackle glaze vase with dancing figure. Longwy, circa 1925. *Lent by Harvey Feinstein for the Finch College Museum Art Deco Exhibition*

Covered box with reclining nude. Longwy for Primavera, Au Printemps, Paris, circa 1925. *Lent by Mr. and Mrs. Peter Brant, for Finch College Museum Art Deco Exhibition*

The general run of British pottery and porcelain in the 1920s and 1930s followed traditional lines and is thus uninteresting to Art Deco collectors. Bernard Leach and Staite Murray, the most important artist-potters of the period, show the influence of Chinese pottery and the English Arts and Crafts Movement of the late nineteenth century. Leach made glazed pottery with bold dot and line designs. Frank Brangwyn, the well-known painter, designed pottery for Royal Doulton, but most of Doulton's output was also reminiscent of the Arts and Crafts Movement. However, a tea set illustrated in the *Studio Yearbook of Decorative Art*, 1920, shows a modern trend in a design of green and black stripes on a white pottery ground of simple form.

The other large manufacturers, including Minton, Royal Worcester, Wedgwood and Copeland, for the most part repeated their old patterns and shapes. Wedgwood did employ the French designer Paul Follot and introduced some squared shapes, but these were not popular. Talbot also designed some important china for Wedgwood. In 1933 Wedgwood brought out a design with diagonal line borders, which was called "Angular Shape." And in 1936 Keith Murray designed a series of pottery vases and cigarette boxes in stepped clear-cut forms of green, white, gray moonstone and buff mat glazes for Wedgwood. The hand-decorated pottery of Alfred and Louise Powell was also fired in the Wedgwood furnaces.

Pottery designed by Clarice Cliff for Newport Pottery had geometric

Porcelain bowl with enameled scene of trees and flowers with dancing girls in leafy costumes holding apples, and animals, birds, and devils in brilliant color. Outside bordered with rectangular medallions of leaping deer. The outside of bowl is decorated with a running scene of the same theme which includes the snake. S. Talbot for Wedgwood, circa 1930. *Jo-Anne Blum, The Antiques Center of America*

decoration of leaves and stylized houses and landscapes in strong green, yellow, orange and black. One design was called Bizarre and was marked "Bizarre, Clarice Cliff, Newport Pottery, England." Clarice Cliff also made a similar pattern of geometric decoration and bold colors for Wilkinson Pottery. This pattern, called Fantasque, is marked "Fantasque, Clarice Cliff, Wilkinson Pottery, England." A pattern called Biarritz was made by Royal Staffordshire. Some lesser Staffordshire companies such as Crown Devon and Midwinter made Art Deco vases and tea sets in squared shapes in the late 1920s and 1930s. The early wares of Midwinter are generally unmarked, but between 1932 and 1944 the marks include the name "W. R. Midwinter, Burslem." The artist Graham Sutherland decorated china for Foley Potteries and China Works, Fenton Longdon, around 1930.

Harold Stabler, who was also a designer of silver, designed Art Deco pottery figures of a goat and a bear. Painted Art Deco candlesticks were also made by Stabler, Adams & Poole. For drawings of marks of these potteries, see *Encyclopaedia of British Pottery and Porcelain Marks* by Geoffrey A. Godden.

Square and stepped forms with zigzag, lightning-shaped handles or solid square and circular handles are seen on teapots, which have motifs of squares, rectangles and circles in transfer designs of black and bold colors.

Whiltshaw & Robinson also made porcelain vases under the trade name of Carlton Ware. They are decorated in colored enamels and gold, and the designs are in floral Art Deco style. There were also many small round, square and rectangular boxes for powder and cigarettes that were decorated in angular Art Deco designs. The hand-decorated pottery of Dora Lunn was made for Ravencourt Pottery.

In the 1920s a group of potters in the Chelsea section of London produced decorative pottery and porcelain figurines. These potters included Harry Parr, Gwendolen Parnell, Phoebe and Harold Stabler, Charles Vyse and others. Most of the figures that are marked with the potters' names are of sentimental subject matter, among them, *The Balloon Women* and *The Tulip Girl* by Vyse. A pottery group consisting of a girl clasping a lamb in her arms and sitting on the back of a fawn is titled *Folies Bergère* and is signed "Charles Vyse, Chelsea." The figurine was sold at Sotheby's in London in the sale of March 9, 1970. Charles Vyse designed a series of figures of this type after 1919. These figures are marked "C. V. Chelsea."

Porcelain vase with enameled fan decoration on iridescent, marbleized red ground. Marked "Carlton Ware (in script) Made in England Trade Mark," circa 1925. Spinning Wheel *Magazine*

In the United States in the 1920s a number of pottery studios grew up in connection with several colleges. One of these, at Newcomb College in New Orleans, produced Newcomb pottery, which is a collector's item today. At Syracuse University there was also an important pottery center, with Adelaide Alsop Robineau the director. The ceramics of Mrs. Robineau, and of Jetta Ehlers who also worked in that locality, are well known today; indeed, the majority of the pieces by Adelaide Alsop Robineau are now in museums. C. F. Binns also established a pottery center at Alfred University, New York, where Syosset pottery was made. In the 1920s George C. Cox, who taught pottery making at Teachers College, Columbia University, was himself a producer of pottery, and in addition to his own output he made designs for several commercial companies. Albert Heckmann of the same college produced his own pottery, vases, boxes and jars for the annual ceramic exhibitions and also designed tea and dinner services for china manufacturers. His designs were usually of conventionalized flowers. The artist Henry Varnum Poor also designed and made pottery. Some of his designs of spiny leaves and flowers are reminiscent of the Wiener Werkstätte. Leon V. Solon was also an important ceramic designer at this time. Cowan, Pewabic and Roseville potteries were all operating in the 1920s, and some of their pottery was modern in both shape and decoration. Their products included vases, plates, lamps, boxes, inkwells and candlesticks.

Signed pieces of pottery and porcelain are good collectors' items. Other pieces should be purchased for beauty of color, form and line if you expect the value to increase.

There are two groups of ceramics made in the late 1920s and early 1930s that should be of special interest to the collector of Art Deco pottery and porcelain who has a limited amount of money to spend; namely, the porcelain figures and household articles put out by Robj and the ceramic sculpture and vases of Robert Lallemand, both of Paris. Lallemand was an individual artist-potter and all his work is signed. In addition to plain angular form vases and candlesticks, he produced such individual sculptural pieces as *Les arbres* and *Château-fort*. In 1928, Lallemand made a series of geometric stepped vases of black pottery. He also made cubistic candlesticks, usually in pairs. Many of his vase forms were hand decorated in red and black or black and green enamel. The designs were cubistic with checkers, cloud and zigzag motifs or with romantic scenes of girls in garden hats and bouffant dresses or sailors in polychrome with the song inscription "Il était un petit navire," and other popular subjects. In 1929 Lallemand made a series of sports sculptures including javelin throwing and cross country races, and a vase with an early train painted in enamel. The vases, sculptures and other pieces are marked "Lallemand/Made in France." Many of the vases were made into lamps, and shades were decorated with designs matching those of the vases. The mounting and the shades were made by Pierre Laville.

## ROBJ PORCELAIN FIGURES

One of the most interesting groups of porcelain bibelots of the late 1920s and early 1930s were made for the Paris dealer Robj. These small figures were designed for display on an étagère, for the table, in the boudoir, for use in the bar or on the dining table. The range of articles was vast, including statuettes, lamps, inkwells, bookends, ashtrays, cocktail shakers, pots for pickles, mustard, oil and vinegar, services for pots de crème, jars for jam and candy, as well as incense burners, liqueur bottles and cigarette boxes.

Robj ceramics are of two types; the amusing utilitarian enameled porcelain figures that were planned to appeal to popular taste and the figures in cream-colored crackled porcelain that were usually designed as decorative statuettes.

The popular decorated porcelain consisted of figures of various countries in their national costumes. Various occupations were also represented, and some figures illustrated popular subjects such as golf, jazz musicians and the opera. These figures were cleverly designed and were often comic as well as ironic commentaries on contemporary life. All these subjects were painted on articles for household use.

The liqueur bottles were some of the most amusing figures. There were ten or more different ones including a coachman, a monk, a policeman, a Scotsman, a three-faced sailor, a Turk with a dagger and a bottle labeled Turkey, a Russian, a figure with Napoleonic hat, a woman with a basket of flowers, an Englishman and an American. Boxes for cigarettes included a figure in Turkish military uniform, an Englishman, an American and Le Caporal. A set of services for pot de crème consisted of six fat stocky figures wearing various types of hats. The mustard and pickle pots were also comic figures and the oil and vinegar bottles were joined figures of clowns. Confitures were covered pots with heads in the shape of different fruits with faces—applies, cherries, pears, peaches—serving as finials on the lids. Candy boxes were sentimental figures in the costumes of Normandy and in other peasant costumes. There was also a box decorated with suites of cards and a figure of a black cat on the lid. Other boxes had busts of maidens and flowers.

A three-piece liquor set consisted of golfing figures. The shaker was the golfer dressed in jazzy sweater and cap, the caddy carried a golf bag holding straws, and a figure of a duck was the lemon

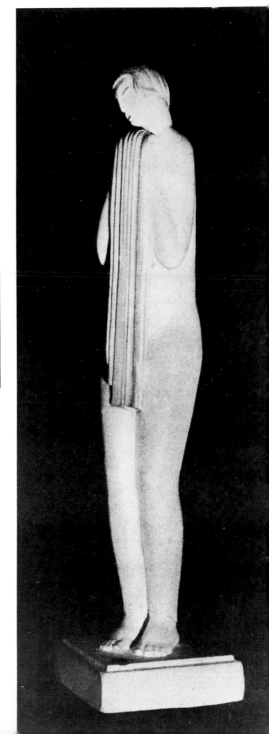

Robj porcelain statuettes. *Above: Poissons* by
Georges Laurent; *Center: Pirogue Indienne;
Right: Nu* by Duprez; Bookends by Coulon,
1927. *From* Mobilier et Decoration, *1927*

Vase of painted faience in cream and brown, hand-signed, and numbered; winner of prize at 1925 Exposition des Arts Décoratifs et Industriels Modernes. Charles Catteau, 1925. *Classic Gallery, New York*

squeezer. Another set consisted of a figure of a butler and six glasses set on a tray. It was designed by Francis Thieck. There were also several amusing tea and coffee services. The tea service "à thé Russe" consisted of a teapot, creamer and sugar, each a Russian figure. These were on a tray with two cups. The pieces of a coffee service had finials of Negro heads.

There were many figures made into incense burners. These included a witch, a peasant, a Japanese and a Turk. But the most unusual incense burners were those with scenes from operas. *Die Walküre* was represented by a figure on horseback; *Carmen* was composed of three figures in characteristic costume; and *Faust* also consisted of three figures including Mephistopheles.

A lamp for the piano was a figure of a cowboy, and statuettes of figures on horses or mules were labeled *Giglio, Taxis* and *Le Roi Rausole*. Each figure is mounted on a rectangular base. A group of four figures with straw bowlers was called *Jazz-argentin*. It was designed by and marked "de Margerie." There were also bookends and ashtrays. Round hand mirrors designed by Francis Thieck have handles in the shape of a gazelle, a duck, and a Pierrot. In 1931, a figure of two dogs, one black and one white, was called *Ric and Rac*. These were dogs in the story "Rab and His Friends," by Dr. John Brown (1858).

Besides such popular humorous figures, Robj produced cream-colored statuettes. These were of modern Cubist-inspired design, and their appeal relied on line and contour as well as subject. In order to interest sculptors and designers in producing figures suitable for these ceramic productions, Robj promoted a competitive exhibition in 1927. Clay models of figures were submitted by recognized artists. The jury consisted of prominent men in the decorative art field: M. Paul Léon, director of the Beaux-Arts and member of L'Institut, assisted by H. M. Magne, president of the Société de l'Art Appliqué aux Métiers, and the artists Landowsky, Dufrène, Pompon, Barthélemy, Bagge, Le-Bourgeois, Georges Saupique and Henri Clouzot, director of the Galliera. The exhibition was held in the new Robj salon, which had been decorated by the designer René Herbst. The first choice of the jury was a statuette by Henri Martin. It consisted of two figures made to hold a mantelpiece clock. The second prize was awarded a figure composition called *Le Chemin de la Vie*. It was composed of three pieces and was by the sculptor Raoul Mabru, professor of sculpture at l'Ecole des Beaux-Arts de Clermont-Ferrand. Afterward this piece was made exclusively for Robj by Manufacture Nationale de Sèvres in a limited edition of twenty. A figure of a cowboy by Pierre Toulgouat won third prize. Other figures included *Drape au Bouquet,* a decorative figure of a woman by Jean Courtebassis; *Le Repos de Diane,* a figure of the goddess with two gazelles by Chauvin, which was also executed in limited edition at Manufacture Nationale de Sèvres, as was the figure *Poissons* by Georges Laurent. Indian figures in a canoe by Mlle Marthe Coulon, and two incense burners, one a turtle by Mme Jeanne Lavergne, the other *Chanteurs de rue,* a group of street singers in the popular vein by Deléage, were also in the exhibition.

The following year Robj again sponsored a competition and exhibition with many of the same distinguished persons serving on the jury. The prizes were awarded as follows: first prize, Noel Feuerstein for a statuette of boats; second prize, Pierre Toulgouat for the statuettes, *Don Quichotte et Sancho;* third prize, Henri Martin for *Tête d'enfant,* a bonbon box. Figures of modern dancers and one of a man with an accordion were also exhibited. A composition called *Helios* was a Cubistic interpretation of a Greek chariot race by Francis Thieck. In 1929 a dancing figure by Mme Guerbe and a nude by Lemanceau were illustrated in *Art et Industrie.* In 1930 nude figures by Maurice Guiraud-Rivière and a Spanish dancer by de Margerie were illustrated in Robj advertisements. In 1931 new figures included a dancer by Bonomé called *Nu pudeur,* airplane sculptures by H. M. Magne, and a figure of three sailors.

Many of the Robj figures were designed by well-known artists and others, some of them excellent designs, were by young artists. Some of the most important artists were Raoul Mabru, sculptor; Henri Martin, a painter of murals who is represented in the Musée de Luxembourg and Musée d'Art Moderne, Paris; Jean Chauvin, Mlle Marthe Coulon and de Hâché were sculptors, and Pierre Blanc, a painter. All are listed in Bénézit, *Dictionnaire Critique et Documentaire.* Robj figures were popular not only in France but in England as well. They were illustrated in French periodicals and in the *Studio Yearbook of Decorative Art* through the late 1920s and early 1930s. Their popularity must have dwindled after 1931 since the advertisements stop at that time. Today the figures are on the market in antique shops and in the Paris Flea Market, and New York dealers are bringing them back from Paris. Robj porcelains are not cheap, but by today's standards they are a good buy, and fun to collect for those

Liqueur bottles: (*a*) Turk holding a dagger and a bottle labeled "Cursky," (*b*) sailor with three faces, (*c*) Scotsman, (*d*) black cook. Robj, circa 1927. *Barry and Audrey Friedman, The Antiques Center of America*

with a limited amount to spend. Many of the decorative statuettes are of excellent design and represent the Cubistic style of Art Deco. Naturally the figures made at Sèvres in limited editions are the most valuable and most difficult to find. All Robj porcelains are marked "Robj" and also "Paris. Made in France." Some liqueur bottles are marked with inscriptions for the kind of liqueur they are made to contain. The decorative figures are marked with the designer's name as well as the Robj name, and some figures are stamped with their titles on the base of the figure in the manner of Victorian Staffordshire figures.

# 7 GLASS

Glass played an important part in the Art Deco period, and there were many makers of glass in France at this time. René Lalique, who had started in the late nineteenth century as a designer of jewelry, headed the list of glass designers of the 1920s and 1930s. Lalique, as a jeweler, often incorporated glass into his jewelry designs, and finally in about 1905, he abandoned jewelry for glassmaking. At first his designs were naturalistic human figures, animals and foliage in Art Nouveau style, but the motifs gradually became more conventional; still later, his designs of vases and lighting fixtures were in the geometric angular forms of Art Deco. For a time Lalique worked, together with the sculptor Gaston Lachaise, in creating glass figures of nudes and animals in tints of blue, brown and peach. The figures were usually of opalescent or frosted glass and were set on a marble or wooden base. His glass maidens are dramatized by hidden light globes. Often, nudes in relief and intaglio also ornamented his clocks; he decorated the faces of other clocks with birds, butterflies and animals. Animals, insects and nude figures were used in relief on vases and other objects as well. A vase with a circlet of nude infants

*Tourbillons.* Molded acid-etched vase carved with high relief scrolls outlined in black enamel. René Lalique, circa 1925. *Cooper-Hewitt Museum of Design, Smithsonian Institution*

*Petrarque.* Vase with large semicircular handles molded in bird and flower design. René Lalique, 1932. *Lent by Cooper-Hewitt Museum of Design, Smithsonian Institution, for the Finch College Museum Art Deco Exhibition*

*Ice Maiden.* Glass on wooden base. René Lalique, 1925. *Lent by Sidney Wordell, for the Finch College Museum Art Deco Exhibition*

Satin-finished vase with leaf borders. René Lalique, circa 1940. *Lent by Cooper-Hewitt Museum of Design, Smithsonian Institution, for the Finch College Museum Art Deco Exhibition*

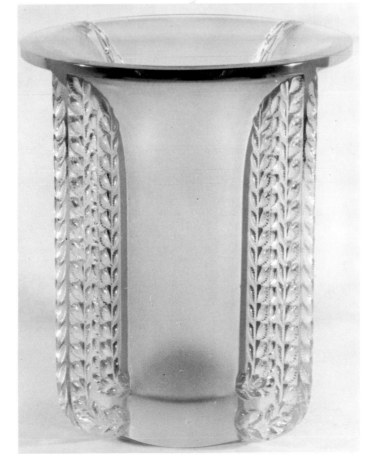

Lalique vases in dull metal tones.
Salon des Arts Décoratifs, 1929

in high relief, made circa 1925, was included in the "Les Années '25" exhibition at the Musée des Arts Décoratifs in 1966.

Circular or semicircular sheets of etched glass were also mounted on marble or bronze bases with concealed electric bulbs. A number of these decorative panels were exhibited in the 1925 Paris Exposition. Lalique globes of glass were also set on marble bases and wired as lamps, and Lalique and Edgar Brandt combined designs of glass and ironwork in attractive floor lamps (see p. 93). Lalique glass was also used for panels concealing wall and ceiling lighting and for glass chandeliers.

Lalique glass was seen in many forms in the various French pavilions of the 1925 exposition. There were fountains and screens of Lalique glass. In the dining room of the Sèvres pavilion, ceiling lights were concealed in panels of Lalique glass and the table and its settings of wine glasses and candlesticks were also designed by Lalique. In the 1930s, Lalique candlesticks were spiral-shaped, with stylized leaves branching from a center stem. In the 1929 Salon des Artistes, a Lalique chandelier consisting of a series of graduated cylinders placed within each other was hung in a dining room by the decorator Henri Rapin.

Since 1908, when Lalique was first commissioned by Coty to design perfume bottles, many small bottles of Lalique design have been made for Coty and for Nina Ricci perfumes. An early perfume bottle, La

*Pavot* scent bottle with red and black molded leaf pattern on clear glass. René Lalique, 1928. *Lent by Cooper-Hewitt Museum of Design, Smithsonian Institution, for the Finch College Museum Art Deco Exhibition*

Libellule, has a dragonfly motif. A scent bottle, Pavot, has a red and black poppy design on a clear glass body. Another bottle has panels of nude figures, and a nude figure of a woman as a stopper. There are also bottles with flower and leaf designs, and the recent bottle for Nina Ricci perfume has one or two frosted doves on the stopper. There was a scent bottle in shades of brown with four women and a bud stopper. A green scent bottle simulating malachite has carving of a nude woman, stylized flowers and a tassel. Another bottle in clear and frosted crystal is decorated with panels of veiled women after the manner of Pompeiian frescoes.

Lalique also made small pieces, such as knife rests in the form of dragonflies, seal stamps with fish bowls and eagles, and radiator caps in the form of a shooting star, a woman with flying hair, and an eagle head that was made for Hitler's marshals.

a

(a) *L'Air du Temps* perfume bottles. *All designed by Lalique for Nina Ricci.* (b) Radiator cap cock. René Lalique, circa 1930. *The Toledo Museum of Art.* (c) Radiator cap dragonfly. Engraved signature "R Lalique/France" (1925–1931). *John Jesse*

c

b

Lalique glass offers many interesting and attractive articles for the collector. Besides the larger more important pieces, figures and lamps, there are small pieces and also dining table glassware. Although the large pieces may be expensive, small perfume bottles, which were made in quantity, are available at reasonable prices.

The finest designs and workmanship are found in the glass made during Lalique's lifetime. However, the glass factory continues in operation today, and many attractive pieces are still being manu-

*Sirene.* Circular dish with molded figure of nude woman and bubbles. René Lalique, 1928. *Lent by Cooper-Hewitt Museum of Design, Smithsonian Institution, for the Finch College Museum Art Deco Exhibition*

factured. There has been a large output of Lalique glass, and some of the most popular pieces, such as the lovebird vase of opalescent glass, have been produced in considerable numbers.

The Lalique molded opalescent glass was imitated, and many such imitations of vases and bowls are found stamped "Etling, France." Etling was a dealer in Paris. He had a shop at 29 Rue de Paradis in the

*Pierrot and Pierrette*. Glass figures. French, circa 1935. *Fred Silberman, The Antiques Center of America*

late 1920s and 1930s and advertised "Bronzes, Céramiques et Terres Cuites, Verreries d'Art" in the magazine *Mobilier et Décoration*. In 1932 there was an article in that magazine on the glass of Etling Cie., illustrating vases and figures made for Etling. These were made of pressed glass from designs by Mme Lucile Sevin, Delabassé, Georges Béal, Géza Hiesz and Mme G. Granger. Illustrated figures that were attributed to Mme Sevin included a ship, *La Caravelle*, and nude figures: *Venus;* Parfums d'Orient, *Le Favori, Delassement, Nu* and *Jeune fille aux cygnes* (a kneeling nude figure with two swans). There was also a fluted vase with standing nudes forming handles, a vase with leaf design and nudes, a vase with a nude figure called *Danseuse*,

*Rampillon.* Yellow molded glass vase, floral decoration amidst raised lozenges. France, signed ''R Lalique/France.'' Circa 1927. *The Corning Museum of Glass*

Glass designed by Mme Sevin for Etling. *From* Mobilier et Décoration, *1932*

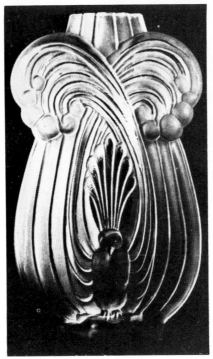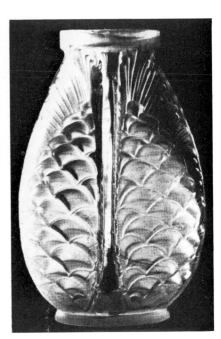

Glass vases. *Left: Femme échevelée* by Mme Sevin. *Center: Oiseaux de Paradis* by Mme Sevin. *Right: Pins* by Béal. All for Etling. *From* Mobilier et Décoration, *1932*

and a vase with a design entitled *Oiseau de Paradis*, which was a conventionalized bird of paradise. Figures by Mme Granger included a three-quarter figure of a mother and child named *En Attendant* and a reclining figure, *Idylle. Danseuse aux Cymbales* was an Oriental figure by Delabassé. There were figures of canaries and a female deer by Géza Hiesz, and swan bookend figures by Béal. A night-light with a group of three lovebirds sitting on a vase of flowers was also by Béal, as was a vase with a pinecone design.

Glass marked "A. Hunebelle," circa 1927, also shows Lalique's influence, although his later glass is angled and geometric in design. By the 1930s Hunebelle had become an important producer of glass. In 1931, Baccarat made a series of glass animal figures designed by the artist–sculptor Georges Chevalier. These included figures of birds, ducks, polar bears, an elephant, a female deer and dogs.

Other important French glass designers of the Art Deco period were the individual glassworkers François Décorchemont, Georges Dumoulin, Maurice Marinot, Henri Navarre, Marcel Goupy and the larger manufacturers such as Daum, Sabino, Genet & Michon, and Cazaux.

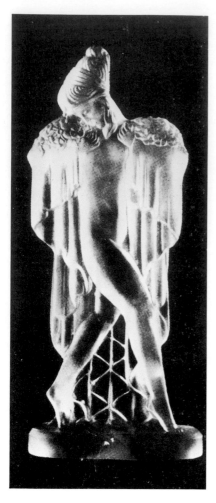

*Parfums d'Orient.* Glass figure by Mme Sevin for Etling. *From* Mobilier et Décoration, *1932*

*Danseuse.* Vase by Mme Sevin for Etling. *From* Mobilier et Décoration, *1932*

Glass bowl. François Décorchemont, 1925 Paris Exposition. *Lent
by the Galleries, Cranbrook Academy of Art, for the Finch College
Museum Art Deco Exhibition*

Nude dancing figure of glass. Cazaux. *Barry and Audrey
Friedman, The Antiques Center of America*

One of these, Maurice Marinot, was an innovator. At first designing forms and painted glass made by other workmen at the Viard glassworks at Bar-sur-Seine, he made his own glass from 1923 on and used manipulating and cutting techniques for decoration. He also modeled his vases and flasks in the furnace, inserting air bubbles and enamel between the layers. His designs are mostly geometrical, the glass gaining its beauty from texture and shape. The textures resemble the bark of trees, snake skin, moss, falling water and cracked ice, whereas other forms are heavy and sculpturesque. Colors include seaweed greens, grays, turquoise, red and a mysterious bistre. Pieces with combinations of green, violet and brown or blues and rose with bubbles remind us of heavy paperweights, but the designs are fluid, creative and imaginative. Some cut and tinted bottles resemble caviar. Marinot worked from 1911 to 1937, and his glass is some of the finest, if not the finest, to be found today. Most of his valuable pieces are in museums. The Daum brothers produced pieces in imitation of Marinot, and Dumoulin and Henri Navarre also made vases in similar style.

Five pieces of glass. *Left to right:* colorless goblet, 1921; enameled goblet, 1919; enameled vase, 1913; bottle with red enamel design, 1920; enameled flacon, 1922. Maurice Marinot. *The Corning Museum of Glass*

Crystal vase with internal red enamel geometric design and deep acid-etched grooves on exterior. Signed Maurice Marinot, 1924. *The Corning Museum of Glass*

a

b

(*a*) glass bottle with stopper. (*b*) glass bottle with grooved cubist design. Signed Maurice Marinot, circa 1925. *Lent by the Galleries, Cranbrook Academy of Art, for the Finch College Museum Art Deco Exhibition*

Glass box with cover. Maurice Marinot, 1931. *Lent by Lillian Nassau, Ltd., for the Finch College Museum Art Deco Exhibition*

Two free-blown perfume bottles of cased glass. *Left:* green, 1936; *right:* purplish brown, 1928. Maurice Marinot. *The Corning Museum of Glass*

Free-blown vase of heavy colorless glass with acid-etched decoration in the form of bosses in deep relief. Maurice Marinot, 1934. *The Corning Museum of Glass*

Glass vase. Daum Frères, Nancy, France, 1929. *Lent by the Galleries, Cranbrook Academy of Art, for the Finch College Museum Art Deco Exhibition*

Jean Luce and Marcel Goupy decorated table glass and toiletware with opaque enamel floral and geometric decorations. Enameled glass was also made by Delvaux. Other pieces of enameled glass have been found marked "Quenvit" and "H. Laroyer." They are usually decorated with cubist roses. Enameled glass was also made by Sabino in Paris. Sabino made vases in white and smoky glass and a great many Art Deco glass vases, bowls, toilet articles as well as opalescent figurines in close imitation of Lalique. These pieces included elephants, roosters, a gazelle and many other figures, including a ballet dancer and a fan dancer. These pieces were modeled by hand and were signed.

Blue glass vase with cut geometric design. Jean Luce, 1929. *Lent by the Galleries, Cranbrook Academy of Art, for the Finch College Museum Art Deco Exhibition*

There were three marks used: incised script, raised block letters and raised script. The small mini-birds were not marked until they were reissued in about 1970. These figures all continue to be made from the original molds, which makes it difficult for the collector to distinguish old from new. However, a yearly souvenir plate was made for the first time in 1970. The plate is signed in incised script and dated on the back "Sabino France Edition Limitée 1970." In 1929 Sabino was

Opalescent nude with drapery and fan. Sabino, 1925–1928. *Collection of Richard Choucroun*

conducting a large business, which included manufacturing lighting fixtures and furniture. Table supports of frosted glass were constructed with concealed lights in the columns.

A large group of Art Deco glass vases, bowls and toiletware bottles and boxes was designed by Legras, Daum and Charder. In Sotheby's sale of March 9, 1970, a cylindrical vase with mottled mauve, gray and orange ground, and a dark mauve circular foot cut with geometric motifs in mauve and yellow, was signed by the artist Charder for Le Verre Français.

Frosted glass vase with enameled scroll decoration. Legras. *Christie, Manson and Woods, Sale catalogue, June 8, 1971*

A small amount of Pâte-de-Verre glass was made in Art Deco design. Pâte-de-Verre was made of powdered glass mixed into thick paste. Layers of this paste of various colors were built up in a mold. When the color and design were finished, the mold was baked in a charcoal oven. The originator of French Pâte-de-Verre was Henri

*Apple Lady.* Pâte-de-Verre vase. Gabriel Argy-Rousseau, 1925–1930. *Collection Minna Rosenblatt*

Isidore Cros, a sculptor, painter and potter who worked at Sèvres. Albert Dammouse, Almeric Walter and George Despreti also created pieces of Pâte-de-Verre early in the century. Lucienne Block in Holland and Frederick Carder of Steuben Glass in the United States made Pâte-de-Verre after World War I. Today Daum at Nancy, France, is producing a few pieces of Pâte-de-Verre from designs by well-known artists. Schneider and Almeric Walter made small pieces, such as ashtrays, birds, bookends, and paperweights. The Pâte-de-Verre glass of Gabriel Argy-Rousseau is the most colorful, and his pieces are the most sought after by collectors. In a recent sale at Sotheby's a bowl of Pâte-de-Verre glass of semitransparent yellow ground with orange and white poppies was signed "G. Argy-Rousseau." Other pieces of Argy-Rousseau Pâte-de-Verre have designs of gazelles and flowers, wolves in a panel with wavy bands of contrasting color or large stylized female heads and a design called the "Apple Lady." Motifs of other Argy-Rousseau glass include masks, satyrs, sea gulls, fish and lions, also such figures as a stylized turkey and a parrot in cream with yellow crest and tail on a base of purple and blue. Argy-Rousseau also made glass and enamel lamps, figurines, cigarette boxes and quantities of floral decorated oval and mask medallions for belts and necklaces. He exhibited in the Salons d'Automne of 1920–1924 and 1934.

François Décorchemont was another artist who experimented with Pâte-de-Verre. But in the 1920s he abandoned the soft glass and subjects of his early days in favor of thick colored glass with geometrical incised floral motifs. His colors are low keyed, including browns, purples and tortoiseshell effects and yellow, green and blue on black glass. He also made figures of stylized turkeys, fish and frogs. In the 1930s Schneider made heavy glass vases in various shapes and sizes, as well as large and small pitchers. He used colors, such as reds shading to orange, orange to yellows, and blues and greens, crystal and smoke. An orange vase is set on a black stand. There is a considerable amount of this glass around and collectors are becoming interested in it because of the beauty of the color. The glass is marked "Schneider," in script.

Talent and imagination were also displayed by the glass designers of Germany, Austria, Hungary and by the Orrefors factory of Sweden and Val-Saint Laurent of Belgium. The Orrefors firm attracted attention at the 1925 Exhibition with its cut glass. Kosta Glasbruk of Sweden made glass designed by Elis Bergh.

In England James Powell & Sons produced glass with cut designs by Gordon Russell that were illustrated in *The Studio Yearbook of Decorative Art*, 1927, and the artist Graham Sutherland decorated glass for Stuart in the 1930s.

In America the finest glass in this period were the rare pieces produced at Steuben by Frederick Carder between 1916 and 1923. Wineglasses and bowls were decorated in blue intarsia with stylized floral sprays. These were signed with Carder's signature, "Fred'k Carder." In the 1930s Steuben produced table glass with engraved Art Deco designs by Walter Dorwin Teague. Since these pieces were mass produced, they are available to collectors today. There are also attractive boxes and vases decorated in black and gold made by Fostoria Glass Co. in this period.

In Vienna, glass with Art Deco patterns was designed by Josef Hoffmann, Dagobert Peche and other designers of the Wiener Werk-

Steuben crystal. Walter Dorwin Teague, circa 1933. *Lent by the Galleries, Cranbrook Academy of Art, for the Finch College Museum Art Deco Exhibition*

stätte. J. & L. Lobmeyer of Vienna made crystal vases with angularly cut designs by the artists Ena Rottenberg and Marianne Roth. The company also made heavy crystal candlesticks, candelabra and toilet sets. Crystal candlesticks in bold angular cut Art Deco designs are available in many shops todays.

The glass of Czechoslovakia is blown, molded and cut, and engraved in striking Art Deco patterns, such as dancing ballet girls, stylized deer and geometric patterns of bold graduating circles. Designs of this type by V. Zahour and Pavel Hlava were shown in the Exhibition of International Contemporary Glass at the Corning Museum in 1959.

Atomizer with etched ruby panels. Czechoslovakia, 1935. *Lent by Barbra Streisand, for the Finch College Museum Art Deco Exhibition*

Enameled glass bowls and vases made in Czechoslovakia in the 1920s and illustrated in the *Studio Yearbook of Decorative Art*, 1926, show angular stepped designs similar to the work of the Wiener Werkstätte. Cut glass was also made with similar designs.

One of the most interesting categories of Art Deco glass collecting is that of blown-glass figures. In the late 1920s and 1930s many figures of animals and humans were made in the glass centers of Italy, Czechoslovakia, Austria and France. The blown-glass music-hall jazz figures of dancing girls and jazz musicians by Léon Zack of Paris are some of the most interesting. Zack combines opaque black and white glass with clear glass. Similar figures were made by the Bimini Werkstätte für Kunstgewerbe in Vienna and by Jaroslav Brychta of Czechoslovakia. One figure shows a man in tails and top hat balancing a cocktail glass in the style of the jazz age.

The perfume bottle is the least expensive and most available category of Art Deco glass collecting. Besides Lalique's, perfume bottles were made by several other well-known glass designers. Maurice Marinot made free-blown perfume bottles of cased glass in green and purplish brown. The shapes were bulky and angular. Gaston Louis Vuitton made perfume bottles in cubist shapes based on Negro art from designs by André Mare, André Groult and Senac. These squat bottles have designs of straight parallel ribs, curved circles and ovals and have ebony or gilt silver tops. Perfume flasks in Art Deco style were also made by Baccarat. One Baccarat bottle has rows of vertical panels, another is decorated with rows of glass scallops. These stylized forms were designed by Georges Chevalier in 1910 and exhibited by Baccarat in the 1925 Exhibition. In 1923 Baccarat advertised a line of decorated glass perfume atomizers.

Cristallerie de Saint Louis and Cristallerie de Nancy perfume bottles in modern cabochon style were on sale in Paris shops in the 1920s and 1930s. An interesting group of perfume bottles was also made in the 1920s and 1930s by De Lettrez for Molyneux perfumes. D'Orsay perfume bottles were designed by Sue et Mare.

Many perfume and dresser bottles are in triangular form or have angular shoulders with triangular stoppers. Perfume flasks and spray bottles were also decorated with angular Art Deco designs of black on clear glass, and some bottles are cut and enameled in black on clear glass. Other bottles are cut and enameled in black geometric designs.

Dogaresse
Robe du soir de Jenny.

Dogaresse. "Robe du Soir de Jenny." George Barbier. From La Guirlande, 1919

*Istar-Sahar.* "Robe orientale de chez Molyneux." George Barbier. *From* La Guirlande, *1919*

*Antinea.* "Manteau de Soir de Paul Poiret." Georges Lepape. *From* Gazette du Bon Genre, *1920*

Marinot glass bottles. *Left:* large deep green bottle with high shoulders. *Center:* angular bottle of purple glass with bright orange-red. *Right:* clear bubble glass bottle in shades of blue. *Lillian Nassau, Ltd.*

*Left:* gold-flecked vase with deeply acid-etched geometric design, signed Muller Frères. *Center:* rose and blue globular vase, signed Muller Frères. *Right:* yellow and orange vase with acid-etched band, Legras. *Lillian Nassau, Ltd.*

*Left to right:* round glass vase on stem, blues with streaks of red, signed Schneider in script; glass pitcher of reds and orange with wine-colored handle, Schneider; large tangerine cup with flecks of deep wine and a deep wine colored stem, Schneider; blue vase with rose-colored floral sprays with deep blue centers, Marcel Goupy. *Fred Silberman, The Antiques Center of America*

Colored etchings. *Left:* red-headed girl in black lace dress with blue bonnet. *Right:* girl with striped skirt and basket of peaches. Louis Icart, circa 1930. *Gladys Koch, The Antiques Center of America*

Lalique bowl with nude figure and tree
branches. 1925/1940. *The Corning Museum
of Glass*

Lalique bottle. 1910/1932. *The Corning Museum
of Glass*

Bottle of free-blown bubbly blue
glass. Maurice Marinot, circa 1923.
*The Corning Museum of Glass*

Group of Marinot glass, free-blown, enameled, and acid-etched. 1919/1921. *The Corning Museum of Glass*

Marinot glass. *Left:* clear bubble glass vase with turquoise diagonal stripes. *Center:* pear-shaped clear glass bottle with inner design of red. *Right:* small clear glass bottle with gold-flecked center core. *Lillian Nassau, Ltd.*

Porcelain figure dressed in bra, shorts, high-heeled shoes and stylized headdress holding pink and green floral shawl. Goldschneider, Austria, 1920/1930. *Fred Silberman, The Antiques Center of America*

Pottery vases. *Left:* bowl with multicolored geometric flowers. *Center:* low bowl with deep blue and turquoise geometric design. *Right:* tall angular vase with panels of blue and turquoise geometric design. Boch, Belgium. *Barry and Audrey Friedman, The Antiques Center of America*

Fauré enamel vases, Limoges, France. *Left to right:* small blue and black vase with diagonal stripes and raised dots; plate with turquoise and white geometric flowers, dark blue accents, and raised dots; large vase with circular design of pinks and reds with black chevrons. *Barry and Audrey Friedman;* small slender-necked red vase with white angular spots accented with black and a pink neck. *Bruce Wendel;* small multilayered pink vase with geometric design in reds. *Gladys Koch*

*Left to right:* small yellow and orange vase with mask in medallion; tall slender vase of light lavender with bands of conventional flowers in circles and wide band of purple with bearded masks of deep coral; bowl of reddish purple with raised white seagulls; large vase of dull orange, yellows and brown with decorative flowers in spirals and raised band of ovals at lip. *Far right:* vase with design of spirals and fish in deep purple, green, and frosted whites. All vases G. Argy-Rousseau. *Barry and Audrey Friedman, The Antiques Center of America*

Glass from Deutsche Fachschule für Glasindustrie, Steinschönau, Czechoslovakia. *Top:* crystal bowl, engraved and painted. *Center, left:* bowl decorated
in colored enamel. *Right:* enameled ruby glass vase. *Bottom:* cut glass vases.
*From* The Studio Yearbook of Decorative Art, *1926*

German glass painted in geometric patterns. Steinschönau, Czechoslovakia. *From* Deutsche Kunst und Dekoration, *1922*

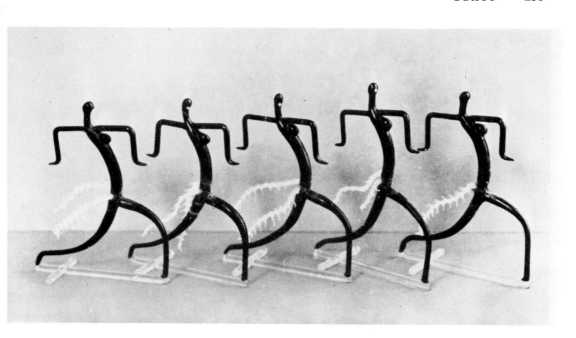

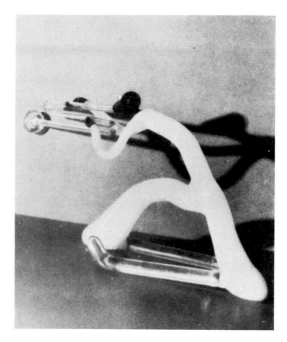

Glass figures. *Above:* black dancers; *below, left and right:* black jazz musicians. Léon Zack. *From* Art et Décoration, *1929*

Perfume bottles. *Back row, center:* large bottle with blossoms by René Lalique; *front row:* small bottles by Viard. *Barry and Audrey Friedman, The Antiques Center of America*

Perfume bottles were also made in Germany, Czechoslovakia, Sweden and other countries. They were made in clear and colored glass and decorated with designs of black enamel.

The collector of perfume bottles might start with some of those now on the market such as the Nina Ricci dove bottle, Guerlain's Vol de Nuit or the high-shouldered Shalimar bottle with the fanlike stopper. The original bottles of these perfumes were first made in Art Deco years. Such bottles as those of Lalique with stoppers of rose garlands or grapes are expensive and difficult to find.

*Hirondelles.* Sculpture of clear, pressed glass on bronze stand. René Lalique,
1926. *The Toledo Museum of Art, Gift of Mrs. Hilliard Rosenthal*

# 8    SILVER

At the beginning of the twentieth century there were design innovators in silver in several countries who helped achieve the balance between form and function. Scottish architect Charles Rennie Mackintosh and the Belgian architect Henry Van de Velde ignored the attraction of Art Nouveau and produced forms that were simple and functional. These men, although not silversmiths, really started the whole modern movement in silver design and influenced the silversmiths of Germany, Austria, Denmark and other European countries.

As the century progressed other designers gradually rejected the traditional and romantic influences of the past and created original forms. By 1910 much of the silverware tended toward simple geometrical forms with practically no decoration. When Art Deco became the style, the forms of silverware kept pace with the other decorative arts of the period, and the silver displayed characteristics of Art Deco. Each nation had a few outstanding silversmiths working in the style of the 1920s and although designs were sometimes similar the silver of each country had its own special character.

In France the important silversmiths of the 1920s and 1930s included Jean Puiforcat, Gérard Sandoz and Jean Serrière. Puiforcat who was a sculptor as well as a silversmith designed silver in restrained cubist forms. His output included tea and coffee services, jars, vases, toilet sets and sets of flatware. He also designed church silver. His pieces are simple in form, based on the square, circle and cylinder. The early pieces of Puiforcat silver are graceful in shape but still related to traditional forms. The usual decoration includes fluting and vertical

Tea and coffee set. Jean Puiforcat, 1925. *Lent by Mr. and Mrs. Peter M. Brant, for the Finch College Museum Art Deco Exhibition*

panels. Handles and finials on such pieces as teapots and coffeepots are often made of wood, ebony or mahogany or of materials such as ivory, crystal, jade or lapis lazuli and the finials may be in the form of a carved flower or fruit. However, as early as 1925, the forms gradually became simpler, heavier and angular. Finials became circles, squares or rectangles. A soup tureen exhibited in the 1925 Exposition is of simple oval form with a circular handle of jade. Puiforcat silver is stamped "JEAN E PUIFORCAT" usually on the sides of hollowware and on the blades of knives.

Tea set with onyx handles and finials. Jean Puiforcat, circa 1925–1930. *Lillian Nassau, Ltd.*

*Left:* silver and crystal vase, Jean Puiforcat, 1925; *right:* silver cigarette box, Emmy Roth, circa 1927. *Lent by Mr. and Mrs. Peter M. Brant, for the Finch College Museum Art Deco Exhibition*

Christofle was one of the old established silvermaking firms of Paris. They manufactured silver pieces from designs of the Italian Gio Ponti and the Danish silversmith Christian Fjerdingstad. In 1923, Christofle exhibited dining table centerpieces with fountains designed by Sue et Mare, and in the 1925 Exposition six pieces of silver designed by Fjerdingstad. In the 1929 Salon des Artistes Décorateurs, Christofle exhibited pieces designed by Jean Serrière, Gaston Dubois and Maurice Daurat. Cardheilhac was another old French silvermaking firm. Their finest work was in the Art Nouveau style and was designed by Bonvallet, although later their designs changed to modern forms.

a

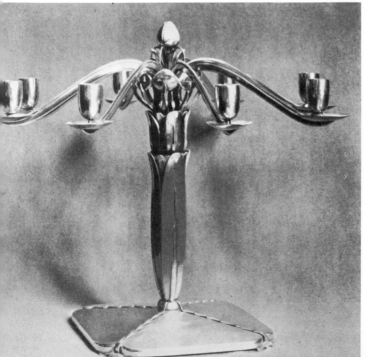

b

(*a*) Silver saucer and covered cup. (*b*) silver candelabra. C. Fjerdingstad, *From* Art et Décoration, *1925*

Silver vase with green decoration. Christofle, 1930. *Lent by the Galleries, Cranbrook Academy of Art, for the Finch College Museum Art Deco Exhibition*

The silver of Têtard Frères is definitely cubist in form. Rectangular boxed shapes in stepped form with flat tops are used for the various pieces of a tea set. The angularity of the form is somewhat relieved by ivory handles and finials. Other French silversmiths of the 1920s included Laparra, A. Rivir, Jean Desprès and Boin-Taburet. Many designers, among them the decorators Maurice Dufrène and Sue et Mare, also made designs for silver that were executed by such firms as Têtard.

a

(a) oval silver bowl with ivory and lapis lazuli. (b) circular covered dish with raised bands. Boin-Taburet, 1925 Paris Exposition. *The Galleries, Cranbrook Academy of Art*

b

Silver table service. Jean Desprès, circa 1930. *Lent by Galerie Sonnabend, for the Finch College Museum Art Deco Exhibition*

Silver sugar bowl with ebony finial and rectangular ebony handles. Body decoration of enamel in tiers of blue and black. Laparra, 1930. *Lent by the Galleries, Cranbrook Academy of Art, for the Finch College Museum Art Deco Exhibition*

Art Deco silver tea set with wooden handles and knobs. French, circa 1930. *Carol Ferranti, The Antiques Center of America*

Danish silversmiths of the era include the famous Georg Jensen, Johan Rodhe, Harald Nielsen, Just Anderson, Kai Bojesen, Laurent Llaurenson, Dragsted and Michelsen and Kay Fisker. Georg Jensen began to design silver in the early years of the twentieth century after first working as a sculptor and a potter. He won recognition as a designer of Art Nouveau silver. The plain forms of the silver are enhanced by leaves, grapes and flowers of openwork design in bases or stems of bowls, within the stems of candlesticks or as finials on the various pieces of a tea or coffee set. The original Jensen pieces are hammered and embossed. Although Jensen is best known for his "grapes and nuts" designs, he also created many simpler designs. Much of the Jensen silver was also designed by Johan Rodhe and Harald Nielsen, and in 1931 Sigvard Bernadotte, son of the King of Sweden, joined the firm and designed for them until 1947. Jensen silver never became cubist in form. The designs have always been based on curves, but the forms are often decidedly modern—of the 1920s and 1930s but never Art Deco.

Octagonal silver tray with design of overlapping concentric circles radiating from outer edges. Laurent Llaurenson, 1929. *The Galleries, Cranbrook Academy of Art*

Silver box. Designed by Kay Fisker and made by A. Michelsen, 1928. *The Galleries, Cranbrook Academy of Art*

Jacob Angman is the best-known Swedish silversmith of the period. He designed for the firm of GAB, the largest silver factory of Northern Europe. Angman's early designs are characterized by the curves of Art Nouveau but later he was inspired by the angles of Cubism. Early coffeepots may have a finial of a dolphin or a fruit, but later finials are of simple circles and squares. The handles are usually straight pot handles of wood.

It was in Belgium that the ornament and fantasy of Art Nouveau silver was first simplified into Art Moderne. As early as 1902 Van de Velde designed teakettles and tea sets that were not to be matched in modern form until a decade later. However, it was Philippe Wolfers and the firm of Wolfers Frères, the Belgian Crown Jewelers, that made the style fashionable. Wolfers exhibited in the 1925 Exposition in Paris. Altenloh of Brussels was also an important Belgian silversmith at this time.

Silver tea set with bud finials, claw feet and ivory handles. Georg Jensen, 1930; original design, 1905. *Courtesy Sotheby & Co.*

Since the eighteenth century most of the German silver has been made in the great centers of Pforzheim, Schwäbisch Gmünd, Frankfurt and Hanau. In the first quarter of the twentieth century the designers Peter Behrens and Richard Riemerschmid influenced the design of silver made in the center at Darmstadt. Both designers pioneered with designs for base-metal kettles, and these simple designs expressing the Jugendstil, or German Art Nouveau style, later influenced the Deutscher Werkbunds. P. Bruckmann & Söhne was the most important large silver company that continued to work in the 1920s and 1930s. Emil Lettre, Josef Wilm and Ernst Schmidt were well-known silversmiths in Berlin at this time. In the late 1930s Michael Wilm of Munich, Theodor Wende of Pforzheim, Wilhelm Binder of Swäbisch Gmünd, Elizabeth Treskow of Cologne and Adolf von Mayrhofer were leaders. They designed silver for churches as well as hollowware for household use.

The silver is characterized by simple forms, the different parts hammered, engraved and mounted or soldered together. The silversmiths of Cologne and Schwäbisch Gmünd are today the most important designers of church silver. Schwäbisch Gmünd is a small village in the Pforzheim district, and when I visited there in 1961 the individual silversmiths worked in their homes, but there was a small exhibit center maintained by the guild.

Although the designs were modern, simple and squared with little ornamentation they were in no sense Art Deco. However, the work of Karl Berthold in Darmstadt was definitely Art Deco and of the type that probably led Graham Hughes, the art director of the Worshipful Company of Goldsmiths, to call Art Deco "undigested geometry."

If there is any silver that can certainly be labeled Art Deco it is that made by Josef Hoffmann, Koloman Moser and Dagobert Peche of the Wiener Werkstätte. This group of artists worked for over three decades designing silver and other articles of gay and frivolous angular design. Hoffmann, the leader and oldest of the group, was to continue to work until his death in 1956. But it was the young Dagobert Peche who seemed to have the fertile imagination and abandon of an Erté, and his silver caskets topped with figures of fanciful female deer or spiked flowers are not only of excellent workmanship but also express the lighter side of Art Deco. Otto Prutscher was also an important silversmith in Vienna in the 1920s and Schmid-

Silver hot water jug. Emil Lettré, circa 1927. *From* The Studio Yearbook of Decorative Art, *1927*

Silver tea set and tray with ebony handles and finials. Wiener Werkstätte, circa 1920. *Parke-Bernet Galleries*

Silver basket. Josef Hoffmann, Wiener Werkstätte, 1910–1915. *Lillian Nassau, Ltd.*

Silver goblet. Dagobert Peche. *From* Dagobert Peche *by Max Eisler*

Silver box with fantastic animal. Dagobert Peche, Wiener Werkstätte, 1920.
*From* Dagobert Peche *by Max Eisler*

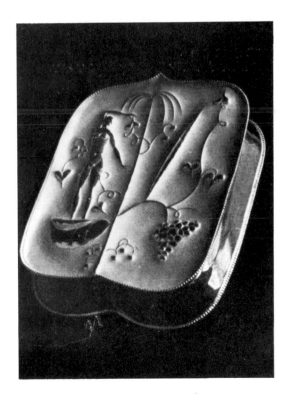
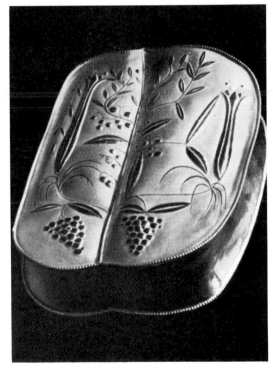

Silver bonbon and tobacco boxes. Dagobert Peche designs, Wiener Werkstätte, circa 1925. *Wiener Werkstätte catalogue*

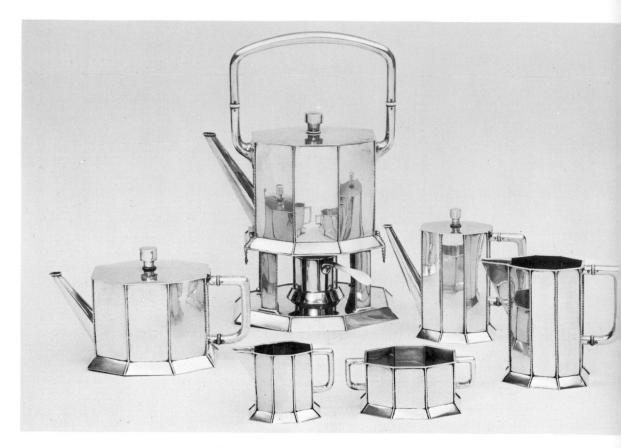

Tea and coffee service of Cubist influence, with beading and ivory bands. Designed by Hans Bolck or Otto Prutscher for Eduard Friedmann Silversmiths, circa 1910. *Fortunoff*

Riegel of Nuremberg also made similar silver caskets and decorative pieces. Numerous small silver tobacco and bonbon boxes were made by the various silversmiths of Wiener Werkstätte. Other Wiener Werkstätte silversmiths were J. Pollak, E. Friedmann and Ernst Lightblau. Still another Viennese designer in the thirties was Friederich Veit.

Meinrad Burch-Korrodi of Zurich, Switzerland, has been designing church silver since 1925. His work, which consists of chalices, crosses, candlesticks, tabernacles, monstrances, wine and water cruets and rings can be found in churches of all denominations throughout the world. Though his forms are simple and definitely modern, they cannot be classified as Art Deco.

The important silversmiths in England in the 1920s and 1930s were Harold Stabler, Harry Murphy, Bernard Cuzner, R. M. Y. Gleadowe,

Silver and coral decorative sculpture of deer and flower. Schmid-Riegel, Nuremberg, 1922. *From* Deutsche Kunst und Dekoration, *1922–1923*

a

b

(a) *The Drunk*. Enamel bowl. (b) Enamel boxes. Friedrich Veit, Vienna, circa 1930. *From* Deutsche Kunst und Dekoration, *1931*

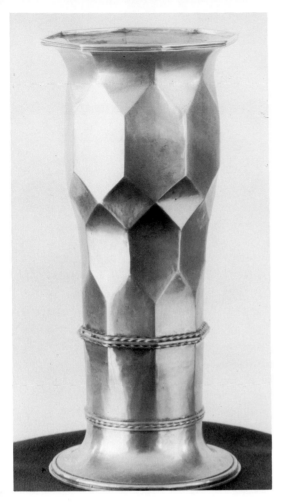

Silver vase with diamond pattern. Omar Ramsden, 1930. *The Galleries, Cranbrook Academy
of Art*

Cluster-column candlesticks. Omar Ramsden, London, 1915.
*Gebelein Silversmiths, Inc.*

Eric Gill and Omar Ramsden. Of these, Harold Stabler is the best
known. His motifs of design include small stepped shapes, zigzag
leaves, cubes and triangles, all inspired by Cubist influence. However, in spite of the modernistic shapes, the pieces seem strangely
traditional. Omar Ramsden is best known for his church silver, which,
although modern and original, is seldom Art Deco.

In America only a small amount of silver was made that could be
classified as Art Deco. A few pieces were made by individual silversmiths, including Arthur Nevill Kirk.

Art Deco silver consisting of spheres and columns was designed
by Eliel Saarinen. Simple vases, bowls and plates without any surface
decoration were also designed by Kem Weber of Hollywood. Weber
also designed candlesticks that were made of other metals.

Tea set. Polygonal with ebony finial and handles. Arthur Nevill Kirk, 1933. *The Galleries, Cranbrook Academy of Art*

Cigarette box of hammered silver with figure blowing bubbles. Eliel Saarinen design, Arthur Nevill Kirk execution, 1933. *Lent by the Galleries, Cranbrook Academy of Art, for the Finch College Art Deco Exhibition*

Vase, sphere mounted on hollow vertically ridged column. Eliel Saarinen, 1935. *Lent by the Galleries, Cranbrook Academy of Art, for the Finch College Museum Art Deco Exhibition*

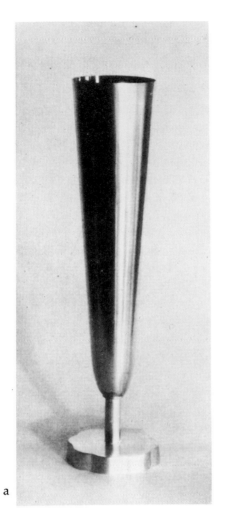

a

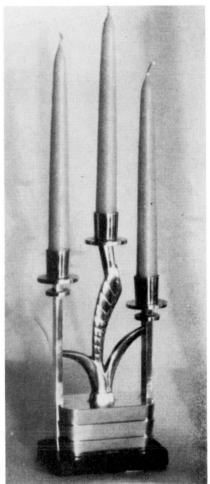

b

c

(*a*) Silver vase. (*b*) Pewter candlestick. (*c*) Silver plate and bowl. Kem Weber, circa 1928. *From* Deutsche Kunst und Dekoration, *1928*

The larger producers of silverware, such as International Silver, Gorham and Tiffany, although they squared, angled and modernized some of their silver, made little that could be called Art Deco. In 1929 International Silver Company made a five-piece sterling silver tea set called Art Moderne. It was of simple form with plain surfaces. The only adornment consisted of oxidized flutes and handles of macassar ebony. In International's 1929 catalogue, silver designs inspired by the modern paintings of Earl Horter, Rockwell Kent and Edward A. Wilson were illustrated. The patterns were named Ebb Tide, Northern Lights and Tropical Sunrise after the titles of the paintings. Another pattern of modified geometric Art Deco design was called Evening Sea. The pieces made in these patterns included bread-and-butter plates, bowls, compotes, console sets with candlesticks, centerpieces for flowers, tall vases, bonbon baskets, relish dishes, mayonnaise sets with matching spoons, almond sets, napkin clips and salt and pepper shakers. International Silver also made pocket flasks, cigarette cases, men's belt buckles and picture frames in engine-turned Art Deco patterns.

Art Deco designs were also used by some of the manufacturers of silver plate and other metals, among them, Wilcox Silver Plate Co., Meriden, Connecticut, and Rogers Bros. The shapes of pieces by Wilcox are definitely angled in Art Deco style. The surfaces are plain with no applied decoration. These are probably the best of the period for collectors. There were compact dinette sets with pieces that fitted into each other on a tray. A four-piece coffee set was of globular

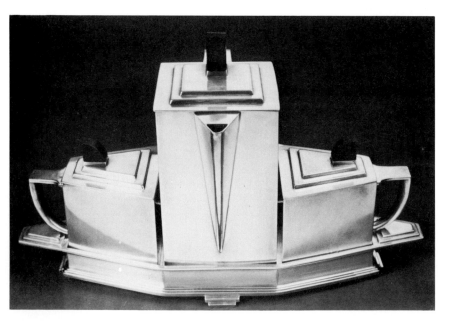

Tea set. Wilcox silver plate, circa 1929. *Frank Weston and Robert Morgan, The Antiques Center of America*

Three vases by Jean Dunand. *Clockwise from left:* vase covered with "Chinée tabac" lacquer, signed; grand vase covered with brown and beige lacquer spirals, signed; round vase decorated with red and black lacquer spirals, signed. *Private collection*

form and sat on an oblong tray. There was also a tea set with tri-angular facets. These sets were silver plated on nickel silver.

Bernard Rice & Sons advertised toiletware of silver and enamel in Skyscraper design in *Jewelers' Circular*, September 20, 1928. In 1930 the International Silver Company advertised silver dresser sets with line decoration of green and black enamel. These sets included mirrors, brushes, combs, manicure pieces, cologne bottles, vanity trays and boxes. The patterns included Contempora silver with three lines of black enamel, Futura with lines of green and blue enamel, Modernique and La Maîtrise. Another design, Les Gazelles, was of engraved deer and leaves with "kinetic contours." The advertisements read: "Modernism is sweeping boldly through the world of art. All our lovely objects are following the new trend of design." Victoria, Picard & Co. also advertised boudoir sets in modernistic design, as did the Elgin-American Manufacturing Company of Elgin, Illinois, in 1928, for their dresser sets, match safes and modern enamel and silver vanities.

Jean Dunand is known for his gracefully shaped vases and plates of hammered metal, which are decorated with simple patterns of inlay

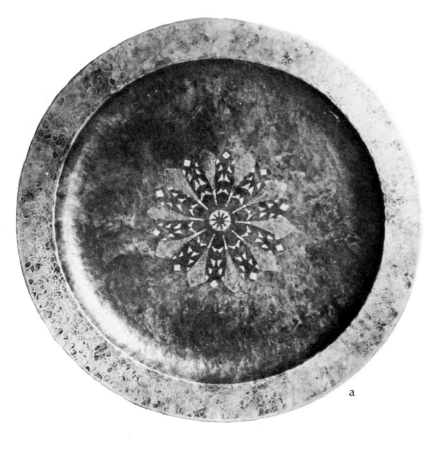

a

b

Copper vase inlaid with silver. Jean Dunand,
1929. *Lent by the Galleries, Cranbrook Academy of Art, for the Finch College Museum
Art Deco Exhibition*

of gold, silver and such metals as zinc, steel and aluminum on a copper
ground. Some vases were covered with coquille d'oeuf lacquer and
enamel. Other vases had red and black lacquer decoration. Dunand
also made vases and trays with designs of gazelles and other running
animals. Dunand was also known for his lacquer plaques, screens and
furniture, which he executed from his own designs and from those of
designers such as Seraphin Soubinin. The designs on screens included
squared line designs, animals and angels and stylized rocks in gold
and silver against black or other colored grounds. Dunand was a
master craftsman, and he is known for his fine workmanship
especially for the execution of the eggshell lacquer, a technique that
he borrowed from the Japanese. Claudius Linossier made metal vases
similar to those made by Dunand. However, Linossier used more
definite designs and geometric motifs including spirals, triangles and
stylized flowers.

c

*(a)* Dish in ferro-nickel, inlaid with copper
and silver, Claudius Linossier. *(b)* Bronze
vase inlaid with silver. *(c)* Lead vase with
acid patina, Jean Dunand. *From* Modern
French Decorative Art *by Léon Deshairs*

Vase, enamel on copper, egg-shell and black. Jean Dunand.
*Barry and Audrey Friedman, The Antiques Center of America*

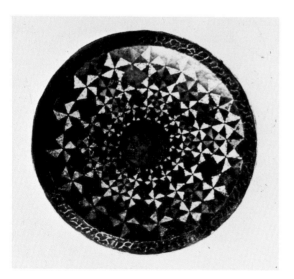 

Plate and vase with bronze and inlaid work. Claudius Linossier, circa 1925.
*From* Modern French Decorative Art *by Léon Deshairs*

Hammered metal vases inlaid with copper and melted silver. Claudius Linossier, circa 1925. *From* Modern Decorative Art *by Léon Deshairs*

Some of the most characteristic Art Deco geometric designs were used on the vases of Sarlandie enamel that were made at Limoges, France, around 1930. The vases have simple cone and cylinder shapes and strong contrasting colors. Multicolored enamel in several layers was laid on the copper base in geometrical patterns. The designs include squares, dots, arrows and silhouette figures. The vases often have rims and bases of silver. Sarlandie enamels were designed by various artists, including Crevel.

The finest of these enamel vases were made by C. Fauré. Vases by Fauré were made in many different shapes, including those of the gourd, kettledrum and egg, with geometric or stylized floral patterns. Geometric designs include chevron, lozenge, diagonal and stripe patterns and floral. Motifs ranged from naturalistic to stylized patterns of leaves and flowers. The geometric patterns are in strong hues of blue, red, orange and yellow accented with blacks, whereas the floral patterns are in more delicate hues such as turquoise, light blue, pink, lavender and white. Some vases have panels and borders of floral motifs combined with geometric stepped and angled motifs.

There are several categories of Art Deco silver or silver plate including electric pocket lighters, cigarette cases, compacts, vanities, mesh purses and dresser sets that are readily available in many shops today. They are usually made of silver with bold Art Deco designs in black, red, orange, yellow and green enamel. Among the American companies that made these items were Ronson Corporation, Elgin-American Manufacturing Company, Eterna Lighters, and Whiting & Davis. Whiting & Davis were the biggest producers of mesh purses and were the first U.S. company to introduce modern designs with triangular borders and bold stripes. In 1928, they advertised an enameled mesh bag with modernistic Poiret designs. Purses by Whiting & Davis are so stamped on the inside of the top frame. The Mandalian Manufacturing Co, of North Attleboro, Massachusetts, also manufactured mesh purses in the late 1920s.

The important Art Deco silver for collectors today is that of Puiforcat in France and Josef Hoffmann, Dagobert Peche and other members of the Wiener Werkstätte. For collectors with small purses there are silver boxes and flatware. Wiener Werkstätte silversmiths were working from 1903 to the 1930s, although Hoffmann worked until his death in 1956. Hoffmann also made flatware and hollowware for Pott of Germany in his later years.

Vase, Sarlandie enamel on copper. Crevel, circa 1930. *Lent by the Galleries, Cranbrook Academy of Art, for the Finch College Museum Art Deco Exhibition*

Sarlandie enamel vase with silver lip and
foot and stylized figures. Limoges, circa
1930. *Lent by Lillian Nassau, Ltd., for the
Finch College Museum Art Deco Exhibition*

Sarlandie enamel vase with silver lip and foot.
Limoges, circa 1930. *Lent by Lillian Nassau,
Ltd., for the Finch College Museum Art Deco
Exhibition*

Sarlandie enamel vase of geometric design with
silver lip and foot. Limoges, circa 1930. *Lent by
Lillian Nassau, Ltd., for the Finch College Museum Art Deco Exhibition*

Vase, enamel on copper geometric design. C. Fauré for Limoges, circa 1930. *Carol Ferranti, The Antiques Center of America*

# 9

# BRONZE AND
# OTHER METAL
# STATUETTES AND
# MEDALLIONS

IN RECENT YEARS THERE HAS BEEN A REVIVED INTEREST IN SMALL ROMANTIC
and realistic figure sculptures of both humans and animals. Along
with this has come a new popularity for the mass-produced casts of
sculpture that flooded the market in the late nineteenth century and
the first quarter of the twentieth century. The shops are again filled
with these bronze and psuedo-bronze statuettes, and the auction room
prices attest to their popularity with collectors.

Small sculpture figures were in demand as a decorative accessory
in the house of the 1890s, and they continued to be used into the
twentieth century. They were set on mantelpieces, on library shelves,
on marble-topped girandoles or wall brackets. Such was the demand
for these figurines that even second-rate sculptors were kept busy
designing these small statuettes for the foundries that mass-produced
the cheap castings.

Many of the figures were made in France, but Austria was also a
center and Austrian taste dominated the design and subject matter of
the earlier pieces, which were close to eighteenth-century traditions.
Trappings of medieval costume, symbolism and the story produced

such romantic figures as the Crusader, the troubadour and figures from Greek mythology.

Art Nouveau influenced a change in subject matter at the turn of the century and nude figures in flowing draperies now became popular subjects. Small bronzes and decorative trifles included candlesticks, lamp bases, clocks, inkwells, and desk sets.

Noted artists who produced ivory and bronze figures in Art Nouveau style include Jean-August Dampt, E. Louis Barrias, Agathon Leonard and Louis Chalon. Dampt produced a figure called *Melusine,* which was composed of an ivory nude in the arms of a man in silver armor. A silver bronze and ivory figure by Louis Barrias is covered with a bronze cloak except for the bust, which is of carved ivory. The jewelry designer Philippe Wolfers also produced figures of ivory and enamel, and a group, *La Caresse du Cygne,* in 1900 shows a bronze swan holding a carved ivory vase. Another Art Nouveau ivory and bronze piece consists of vines holding a group of candle sockets that cradle a nude ivory figure.

Early in the twentieth century Gallé made lampshades for lamps with bases of bronze and ivory. The bases were signed P. Tereszizuk. Other bronze figural lamps and bronze desk sets, which were a combination of bronze and carved ivory, were also marked P. Tereszizuk. Art Nouveau bronze and ivory statuettes of figures in Neo-Gothic robes were also signed "Raphond." Other designers of bronze and ivory figurines at the beginning of the twentieth century include L. Barthélemy and Alonza. Many of the small bronze statuettes put emphasis on the nude or draped figure in preference to medieval costume, but many of them also used the Pierrot and Columbine theme and characters from literature and drama.

Bronze inkwell with carved ivory face within the eye of the peacock feather. Signed P. Tereszizuk. Art Nouveau, circa 1915. *A. Christian Revi and* Spinning Wheel *Magazine*

The exotic scarf dancer Loie Fuller was an enormous success in Paris. The sculptor Agathon Leonard inspired by her dancing designed a series of eight dancing figures, *Le Jeu de l'Echarpe*, which were made in Sèvres biscuit porcelain and exhibited at the Paris 1900 exposition. These were later cast in bronze by Susses Frères. The casts are found in several sizes, and are signed A. Leonard, Sculp., together with the foundry mark. There were also gilt-bronze figures and a lamp by Raoul Larche in the form of Loie Fuller with folds of her silk drapery swirling round her.

Early in the twentieth century Art Nouveau began to extricate itself from the tangle of historicism. Whereas the Cubists and other contemporary groups hit at the inner structure, the influence of speed, dynamism and the machine was evident in sculpture design before World War I. Human and animal forms became dramatically stylized. The sunray and the rainbow motifs were already established. Also, nude figures, together with gazelles, greyhounds, and flowing scarfs, as seen in the sculptures of Paul Manship, were particularly popular. In fact, the themes and stylization of Manship's early sculptures, such as *Salome*, 1915; *Flight of the Night*, and *Dancer and Gazelles*, 1916, are seen repeated again and again in the mass-produced sculptures of the era that began to flood the market.

The production of small bronzes was interrupted by the war, but in about 1920 they were again made in quantities and they continued popular throughout the 1920s and 1930s.

The sculptors Marcel Bouraine, P. le Faguays, G. H. Laurent and Gennarelli were producing stylized straining figures with flowing hair. These were sold in New York in such high quality shops as Alfred Dunhill in the early 1920s.

Bronze figure. Signed Marcel Bouraine. *Barry and Audrey Friedman, The Antiques Center of America*

*Fame.* Bronze figure. P. le Faguays. *Barry and Audrey Friedman, The Antiques Center of America*

## BRONZE AND OTHER METAL STATUETTES

In the 1920s the Gorham Company operated a bronze division with foundries at Providence, Rhode Island, and also maintained exhibition galleries at Fifth Avenue and Forty-seventh Street, New York City, where their stock of sculptures was displayed and sold. These sculptures included small figures of animals, men, women, children, as well as such articles as bookends, all by well-known American sculptors. In their 1928 catalogue, the sculptors included Emilio Angelo, Chester Beach, Gutzon Borglum, Allan Clark, Mabel Conkling, Cyrus E. Dallin, Frank E. Dodge, Abastenia Eberle, Laura Gardin Fraser, Harriet W. Frishmuth, Emil Fuchs, Karl Gruppe, Anna Hyatt Huntington, Maude S. Jewett, Bernard P. Johnson, Isidore Konti, Robert Tait McKenzie, Bonnie MacLeary, Edith B. Parsons, Margaret Postgate, A. Phimster Proctor, Lucy C. Richards, Philip Sears, Julie Nichols Yates and Mahonri Young.

The most popular figures were the small nudes by Harriet Frishmuth. These figures were available as statuettes or as life-size table fountains. A small nude called *Vine* was a miniature edition of a life-sized statue owned by the Metropolitan Museum, and a dancing figure, Desha, was of the dancer who was the model for many of the other figures. All these figurines had a green patina and were mounted on black Belgian marble bases.

*Study of Two Dancers.* Table fountain by Maude Sherwood Jewett for Gorham, circa 1920s. *George Schwartz, The Antiques Center of America*

Other nude figurines in the Gorham collection included *Forever Young, Forever Panting,* and *Bedaja Dancer* by Allan Clark, *Glint of the Sea* by Chester Beach and *Joy of Life* and *Butterfly*, a small figure with a butterfly alighting on her heel, by Emil Fuchs. There are also chubby figures of children, such as *Turtle Baby* and *Duck Baby* by Edith Parsons and *Moon Fish* by Mabel Conkling, and *Ouch*, a tiny figure of a child with a turtle biting its finger, by Bonnie MacLeary. These figures were available in large sizes for fountains, and some were arranged as flower holders.

Goats. Bronze bookends. Anna Hyatt Huntington. *George Schwartz, The Antiques Center of America*

Two Indian figures by Cyrus Dallin, *Appeal of the Great Spirit* and *Scout*, and a finely modeled bronze, *Bronco Buster*, signed Maurice Guiraud-Rivière and showing the influence of Frederic Remington, represent themes relating to the West that were especially popular with the general public at this time.

Bronze bookends included elephant figures by Mahonri Young, goats by Anna Hyatt Huntington and of men pushing by Isidore Konti.

Animal figures included panthers, tigers, a great Dane and the horse *Morgan Stallion* by A. Phimster Proctor. *Joan of Arc* by Anna Hyatt Huntington, the original of which is in a private collection on Riverside Drive, New York City, was available in two sizes: fifteen inches and fifty-one inches.

The catalogue also includes a radiator cap entitled *Speed*, which shows a forward-stretching figure with streaming hair, wings and outstretched hands. It is silver electroplated over bronze and was made in two sizes: four inches high by eight inches long and six inches high by twelve inches long. It was designed by Harriet Frishmuth. Only about forty of this rare piece were made.

Gorham art bronzes were marked with the name of the sculptor and the Gorham bronze mark, a rectangle divided into three sections with *G* in a square at one end, *C* in a square at the other end and a figure of a panther in a rectangle in the center. The number of castings ranged from twenty-five to over two hundred.

The most popular bronze and ivory figures portrayed the life of the 1920s including the sports, the night life and even the fashions. It is easy to establish the dates when these figures were made because of their subject matter. The largest group of figures are of dancers who illustrate the popular dances as performed in the Paris nightclubs: the ballet dancer, the torch dancer, the fan dancer, the spider dancer, the bat dancer, the Apache dancer, the Russian Cossack, a snake dancer and the expressionist dancer. All these dances are portrayed by figures of bronze with ivory heads and hands. Some figures are also decorated with colored enamel. Another group of figures illustrates sports:

Bronze figure. Signed D. Chiparus.
*Gladys Koch, The Antiques Center of America*

Bronze figure of a dancer with ivory head and hands (figure available in several sizes). Signed D. Chiparus. *Gladys Koch, The Antiques Center of America*

tennis, bathing, skating and archery. Tennis was the most popular and there are a number of excellent figures that illustrate this sport. The cowboy theme was also popular. Many of the figures were copies of earlier sculptures. There were Siamese and Cambodian dancers with swirling skirts, Neo-Gothic figures in medieval costumes, Salome, Arab horsemen and Mercury.

There were also figures of harlequins and clowns playing mandolins. But some of the most interesting figures are the gay Parisian cocottes with bobbed hair, dressed in trousers, long fitted jackets, cloche hats or hair in banderole and wearing exotic jewelry. An amusing bronze and ivory gamine, with high heels and clinging trousers, shirt neckerchief and peaked cap, poses with her hands in her pockets and smokes a cigarette. Dancing girls in tunic or bikini and turbans balance on one leg with outstretched arms. Others wear long-waisted dresses with bateau or V neckline, full circular skirts longer in the back and trimmed with several rows of ruffles, bowknots or ostrich feathers. All these figures stand on marble bases, circular, square, triangular or stepped. The majority of the figures are signed by the artist, in the bronze or on the marble base. The following is a list of the most important sculptors of these subjects whose figures have come on the market in the last year or so:

| | |
|---|---|
| ADOLPHE | P. LE FAGUAYS |
| ALONZO | S. LIPCHYTZ |
| L. BARTHÉLEMY | LORENZL |
| BEQUERELLE | R. PARIS |
| D. CHIPARUS | P. PHILIPPE |
| C. COLINET | F. PREISS |
| GERDAGO | G. RIGOT |
| G. GORI | ROLAND |
| MAURICE GUIRAUD-RIVIÈRE | SWIN |
| JACQUEMIN | BRUNO ZACK |
| P. KOVALEZ | |

Silvered bronze and ivory figures on onyx marble plinth. *Left:* bat dancer; *right:* tennis player. F. Preiss, late 1920s. *Parke-Bernet Sale Catalogue, April 27, 1971*

Bronze and ivory figures. *Top left:* archer with gilded tunic and red kerchief on onyx plinth and black marble base, signed F. Preiss. *Top right:* torch dancer in silvered bronze bloomers on truncated onyx marble plinth, inscribed P. K. (P. Kovalez). *Above:* two bronze figure skaters on truncated marble base, signed Jaquemin. *Parke-Bernet Sale Catalogue, January 28, 1971*

Bronze figures. *Left:* figure of girl in jacket and trousers painted silver and gold, with ivory head, signed G. Gori. *Center:* ivory figure with gilded bronze drapery and onyx base, signed S. Lipchytz. *Right:* bronze figure on onyx base, Lorenzl. *Fred Silberman, The Antiques Center of America*

Bronze figure of two girls in party dresses with head and arms of carved ivory.
Signed Sevin, circa 1920. *Fred Silberman, The Antiques Center of America*

Bronze nude with veil. P. Philippe. *Barry and Audrey Friedman, The Antiques Center of America*

Bronze figure of woman and greyhound. Cloak enameled with gold flowers, hands and face of carved ivory, signed Bequerelle. *Fred Silberman, The Antiques Center of America*

These miniature sculptures have been sold principally in jewelry shops and in gift shops. An article "Miniature Sculpture in Bronze and Ivory," which appeared in the American magazine *Art in Trade* in April 1929, indicates their popularity at that time, and these miniature sculptures in bronze and ivory continued in popularity into the 1930s as is evidenced by an article in *Jewelers' Circular-Keystone*, January 1935. The article is signed by M. Applebaum, a member of the firm of Friedleander Co., Inc., a company that sold bronze and ivory sculptures and other works of decorative art. The author writes: "Vast new potentialities in the field of small sculpture and in the way of increased naturalism have been made possible by the modern treatment of bronze and ivory alone and in composition." After the statue is cast it

must now be plated, colored or patinaed in accordance with the artist's conception. The Florentine and Spanish work of this type has from its beginning been known for its beauty, and today the bronze statuettes, based upon these, and in fact upon every style of bygone days are produced in great quantity. Many copies of antique work are so skillful that it is difficult for experts to detect their origin.

Unconventional and fresh ideas are undergoing continual experimentation, and it is the custom to leave the original handiwork of each designer untouched. Blending colors are used upon bronze, the glitter of which has been subdued by means of patinas and oxides. A special shell is sometimes introduced to replace ivory and enameling adds to the finish of certain designs.

The quality and workmanship of the ivory carving varies. Many of the ivory inserts may have been made by different craftsmen from those who designed the bronze, or perhaps the bronze worker was not skilled in ivory carving. However, the former supposition seems more probable since the ivory in pieces by the same bronze sculptors seems to vary in carving.

By the 1920s new processes of manufacture and substitutes for true bronze allowed for figures to be mass-produced at small cost, and cheap figures made of combinations of metal alloys flooded the market.

One of the sources for these figures was the Paris artist-editor Max le Verrier. Le Verrier produced "Objets d'Art Fontaines, Luminaire" designed by himself and other name artists. These articles were sold in

*Groupe Séduction.* White metal figures. Signed Fayral. Catalogue of Max le Verrier, Paris, 1925. *Vincent Primavera, Florentine Craftsman*

his shop at 100 rue du Théâtre in Paris and also consigned to shops in England and America. Le Verrier issued a catalogue in 1925. In the catalogue were statuettes, lamps, incense burners, bookends and ashtrays. These figures were cast in white metal, a mixture that was mostly zinc. The figures, which resembled bronze, were mounted on marble bases, and the metal was sometimes combined with ivory and semiprecious stones. The largest group of figures was of nudes dancing or posed with veils in various graceful positions. There are also nude figures holding glass bowls with hidden lights. One lamp consists of two nudes holding a drapery that supports a basket of glass flowers in which a light globe is concealed. Other figures have such titles as *Moyen Age; Pégase; L'envoi; Frileuse au tub; Bacchanale; Farandole; Printemps; Atlante; Amazon au javelot* and *Olympie.* There are animal figures including monkeys, pelicans, squirrels, eagles, bison, goats, gazelles, hounds, a bulldog and cats. Many of the animal figures are made into bookends and ashtrays. A group of hounds titled

*Left and right:* white metal figures of deer. *Center:* Icarus, bronze figure on onyx base. *Frank Weston and Robert Morgan, The Antiques Center of America*

*Danseuses au voile.* Terra-cotta figures. Signed le Faguays. Catalogue of Max le Verrier, Paris, 1925. *Vincent Primavera, Florentine Craftsman*

*La soif au désert* won a prize at the Salon des Artistes Décorateurs, and a figure of a monkey under an umbrella was exhibited at the Salon des Humoristes. Max le Verrier signed his pieces "M. le Verrier." Other artists illustrated in the catalogue include: Fayral, Janle, Artushaut, Laurent, de Marco, Charles, Derenne, Denis, Guerbe, Bouraine, Masson, Raph, Scarpa and le Faguays. All pieces were signed. An advertisement of Max le Verrier in *Art et Industrie*, May 1930, illustrated a dancing nude with a panel of drapery holding a large fan in back of her head.

Wrought iron bookends: leaping gazelles. Gilbert Poillerat.

Beginning in 1920 there were many dealers in New York selling small bronze and other metal sculptures. There were also small companies producing these figures for use on lamps, bookends and ashtrays. One of the companies most active in this work was Frankart. Although they made vases, ashtrays, clocks, bookends and boxes, the largest part of their business consisted of lamps. The lamp globes were upheld by cast-metal nude figures in graceful poses and were wired for electricity. The metal figure could be ordered in several different finishes: "Roman green, Jap black and French bronze finish." Glass on some lamps could be either prismatic crystal or amber. A nude figure standing on her head and balancing a black glass ball with her toes was patented in 1928. The glass ball was also available in champagne or green glass. It had a concealed electric globe. Other lamps were available with glass cylinders of canary, orange, red, flame or white. A clock of rectangular frosted glass illuminated at the back and flanked by two nude metal figures and set on a rectangular stepped stand was advertised in 1929. Lamps had one or two nude metal figures upholding circular or rectangular stepped glass lights. Other lamps had figures holding frosted and fluted cylinders of glass. A Bubble Ball lamp with a crystal ball was advertised in 1929, and a cube lamp with two seated nudes flanking a cube of colored or crystal glass was advertised in 1930.

Frankart was only one of the many manufacturers and dealers that produced metal figures. Pompeiian Bronze produced commercialized sculpture such as cowboys, Indians, pirates, wild horses and dogs. They made figures of a desert sheik, a broncobuster and an Indian on a horse. These figures were also used as bookends and as decoration on alabaster ashtrays, boxes and novelties. In 1929 Pompeiian Bronze advertised a series of bookends with figures of Rip Van Winkle, Robinson Crusoe, Gold Digger, Buccaneer, Pirates' Den and a Remington-like figure of a man on a horse. These figures were all made of cast white metal with psuedo-bronze finish. Some were made of plaster with a metal coating.

Other companies that made similar commercial figures included Janusch Mfg. Co. and Armor Bronze Co. J. B. Hirsch was also an importer and manufacturer. Rustic Well Foundry of Bridgeport, Connecticut, and S. S. Spencer's Sons of Guilford, Connecticut, also made art bronzes. Spencer's small figures were original and amusing. One figure called *Hurdler* shows a figure on a horse taking a hurdle. Another figure, *Lucky Luke,* was a Disney-like duck. The figures are marked with the Spencer trademark. These bronzes were finished in gold, silver or light green. However, many of the commercialized sculptures were unmarked. These small figures of dogs, deer, cowboys, Indians and pirates, as well as those of stylized nudes, flooded the American market in the 1930s. They were the stock of the gift shop and were on the list of every Christmas shopper. Those that didn't get thrown in the ashcan are in the thrift and the antiques shops today. They were cheap when made, usually under ten dollars, and should not be priced above that figure now.

There are many good bronze figures available today. The material can be checked by scraping the underside with a knife. The bronze casting should be judged by the quality of its casting and by the sharpness of its detail and modeling. Sculptures with ivory details also vary in quality. Although many of the sculptors who signed these figures were members of the Salon des Artistes Français and are listed in Bénézit, they were completely ignored by the art literature of the period, and are not mentioned in books on art history. However, just as art historians and museums finally got around to the Victorian era, now that Art Deco is recognized, it is time for a revaluation of the figures by sculptors such as Chiparus, Preiss, Zack and other sculptors of bronze figurines of the 1920s and 1930s. For the collector, the prices are already soaring, but with patience and search one may still find some bargains.

## BRONZE MEDALLIONS

Another category for the collector of medals is that of bronze medallions. Bronze medallions were made in Europe from early centuries, although their present forms probably date from the Renaissance. For the collector of Art Deco, the medallions made for the Exposition Internationale des Arts Décoratifs of 1925 are a starting point. These

Bronze medallion: 1925 Paris Exposition. Pierre Turin

*Le Secret du Bonheur.* Bronze medallion. Jean Vernon, circa 1935

*Abundance.* Bronze medallion with female supporting floral offering. Pierre Turin

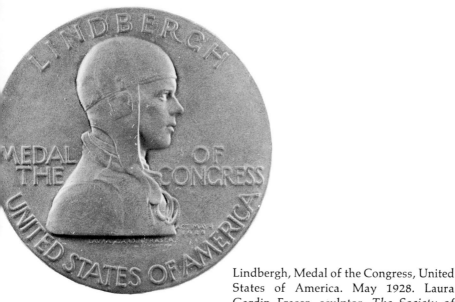

Lindbergh, Medal of the Congress, United States of America. May 1928. Laura Gardin Fraser, sculptor. *The Society of Medalists*

include medallions by Pierre Turin, Dammann, Marcel Renard and Jean Vernon. Among the medallions designed were those for the maiden voyages of the French liners *Paris, Ile-de-France* and *Normandie,* and one for the Défense du Canal de Suez in 1930.

The early beginnings of the American medallion can be traced directly to France. In fact, the first American commemorative medals for the heroes of 1776 were made in France. After the War of 1812, medals were made at the mint in Philadelphia from sketches by engravers, and during the first half of the nineteenth century the medallic art was tied to the Philadelphia Mint. By the mid-nineteenth century sculptors began to be interested in designing medals. The American sculptor Augustus Saint-Gaudens, who studied at the Ecole des Beaux-Arts in Paris, promoted the interest of the American public in the medal as an art object in miniature. At the turn of the century the Medallic Art Company was founded in New York by two Frenchmen. In the sixty-seven years of its existence the company has worked to develop and stimulate the artistic talent of the American sculptor. Some of the famous American sculptors from whose works medallions have been made include Augustus Saint-Gaudens, Victor D. Brenner,

General Motors 25th Anniversary medal, 1933. Designer, Norman Bel Geddes; René Chambellan, sculptor. *Medallic Art Company*

City Club of Denver Fine Arts Award medal, 1928. Arnold Ronnebeck, sculptor. *Medallic Art Company*

Laura Gardin Fraser, James Earle Fraser, Herbert Adams, Chester Beach, John Flanagan, Anthony de Francisci, Robert I. Aiken, Lee Lawrie, Hermon A. MacNiel, Paul Manship and Brenda Putnam.

After the First World War American sculptors produced several commemorative medals. In 1920 John Flanagan designed a medal for presentation by the people of the United States to the city of Verdun, France. Chester Beach designed a medal at the time of the Peace of Versailles in 1919, and Daniel Chester French made an American Red Cross medal in 1920. Laura Gardin Fraser designed the medal dedicated to the chaplains of the American Army in 1920.

American medals of the 1920s that would be of interest to the collector of Art Deco include the following:

Kansas City Art Institute Medal, 1925. 2-inch bronze, gold, gold-filled, silver. Wallace Rosenbauer, sculptor.

Manhattan Purchase Tercentenary Medal, 1926. 2½-inch bronze, silver. Hermon A. MacNiel, sculptor. American Numismatic Society.

Southampton Hospital School of Nursing Medal, 1927. 1½-inch bronze, gold plated. Man and sun's rays. Laura Gardin Fraser, sculptor.

Pennsylvania Museum and School of Industrial Art Medal, 1927. 1¾-inch bronze, gold. Woman with flowing hair. John R. Sinnock, sculptor.

Tiffany Foundation Medal, 1927. 3-inch bronze, silver. Straining nude figure with wings. Edmond Amateis, sculptor.

New York Central System Valor Medal, 1928. Robert Aitken, sculptor.

Guggenheim (Daniel) Medal, 1928. 2½-inch bronze, gold. Airplane in flight. Theodore Spicer-Simson, sculptor.

City Club of Denver Fine Arts Award Medal, 1928. 3-inch bronze, silver. Art Deco design of clouds, sun's rays and stepped buildings. Arnold Ronnebeck, sculptor.

General Motors 25th Anniversary Medal, 1933. 3-inch aluminum, bronze, silver plate, silver. Design of contemporary plane. Norman Bel Geddes design. René P. Chambellan, sculptor.

The above medals were all cast by Medallic Art Company.

*Hail to Dionysus.* Bronze medallion. Paul Manship, 1930. *The Society of Medalists*

In 1930 the Society of Medalists was organized. Its goal was the encouragement of the medallic work of American sculptors and promoting the recognition of the artistic medal by the public. The first group of medallions sponsored by the Society of Medalists included Paul Manship's *Hail to Dionysus*, 1930. Other medallions sponsored by the Society in the 1930s include the following:

| NO. | DATE | SCULPTOR | OBVERSE | REVERSE |
|-----|------|----------|---------|---------|
| 1 | 1930 | Laura Gardin Fraser | *Hunter & Dog* | *Turkey* |
| 2 | 1930 | Paul Manship | *Dionysus* | *Satyrs on winepress* |
| 3 | 1931 | Hermon A. McNiel | *Indian prayer for rain* | *Hopi Indian dance* |
| 4 | 1931 | Frederick MacMonnies | *Charles A. Lindbergh* | *Lone Eagle allegory* |
| 5 | 1932 | Lee Lawrie | *Whatsoever man soweth* | *He shall also reap* |
| 6 | 1932 | John Flanagan | *Aphrodite* | *Swift runners* |
| 7 | 1933 | Carl Paul Jennewein | *Gloria (glory)* | *Fama (fame)* |
| 8 | 1933 | Gaetano Cecere | *No easy way to stars* | *Difficulties of life* |
| 9 | 1934 | Herbert Adams | *Youth fishing* | *Fish as prize* |
| 10 | 1934 | Albert Laessle | *America (turkey)* | *Abundance (corn)* |
| 11 | 1935 | Lorado Taft | *Great Lakes* | *Daughters of Danaus* |
| 12 | 1935 | Anthony de Francisci | *Creation* | *Swirling universe* |
| 13 | 1936 | R. Tait McKenzie | *Athletics (shot put)* | *Runners* |
| 14 | 1936 | Albert Stewart | *Savagery of war* | *Peace* |
| 15 | 1937 | Robert I. Aitken | *Love is immortal* | *Love creates beauty* |
| 16 | 1937 | Chester Beach | *Peace* | *War* |
| 17 | 1938 | A. Stirling Calder | *Dance of Life* | *Pleasure, pain* |
| 18 | 1938 | Gertrude K. Lathrop | *Conserve wildlife* | *Antelope* |
| 19 | 1939 | Edward McCartan | *The new world* | *The old world* |
| 20 | 1939 | John Gregory | *Ceres' blessing* | *Scarcity . . . shun you* |

These medals were also made by the Medallic Art Company.

*Creation.* Bronze medallion. Anthony de Francisci, American, 1935. *The Society of Medalists*

*Peace.* Bronze medallion. Albert Stewart, American, 1936. *The Society of Medalists*

Art medals may be collected for their design, for the sculptor who made them, for different sculptural techniques, different materials, for unusual patinas or for rarity. But what makes art medals distinctive is the fact that, instead of being made from engraved dies, they are made from models prepared by sculptors from original designs worked in clay and transferred to plaster. The sculptor's model is reduced in scale and multiple struck or cast to reproduce all the original detail, and given a patina to highlight and emphasize the sculptor's original design.

# 10 GRAPHICS AND POSTERS

ART DECO GRAPHICS ARE WORTH A BOOK TO THEMSELVES, NOT JUST A BRIEF chapter. They include posters, book illustrations, typographic ornaments, bookplates, greeting cards and advertisements, such as stamp books. Their subject matters include landscapes, portraits and geometric abstractions. In technique, they range from lithographs to woodcuts, in black-and-white and color.

## BOOK ILLUSTRATION

Book illustration offers an interesting field for the collector of Art Deco. Black-and-white lithography, etching and block prints were especially popular at this time, and their bold angular designs expressed the spirit of the times. In America, Lynd Ward, John Vassos, Ralph Pearson and Rockwell Kent were among those who illustrated books in the 1920s and early 1930s. Rockwell Kent also designed bookplates, posters, Christmas cards, book jackets and advertisements. The books he illustrated include *Architectonics: The Tales of Tom*

*The Flame.* Wood engraving by Rockwell Kent, 1928. *The Cleveland Museum of Art, Dudley P. Allen Fund*

*Thumbtack, Architect* (85 illustrations and initial letters), 1914; *Rollo in Society: A Guide for Youth* by George S. Chappell (19 illustrations by Hogarth, Jr. [pseudonym of Kent]), 1922; *A Basket of Posies*, verses by George S. Chappell (pictures by Hogarth, Jr.), 1924; *The Memoirs of Jacques Casanova* (12 drawings), 1925; *Dreams and Derisions—Nineteen-Twenty-seven* (65 illustrations and decorations); *Candide* by Jean François Marie Arouet de Voltaire (81 illustrations), 1928; *Moby Dick* by Herman Melville (280 illustrations), 1930; *Venus and Adonis* by Shakespeare (21 illustrations in black and red), 1931; *City Child*, poems by Selma Robinson (42 decorations); *The Bridge of San Luis Rey* by Thornton Wilder (7 lithographs in color), 1929; and *Beowulf* (8 lithographs and initial letters), 1932. Rockwell Kent also did advertisements for Marcus Jewelry and the American Car and Foundry Company.

Lynd Ward's black-and-white woodcuts for *God's Man* tell the story boldly and satirically. Ward also illustrated Goethe's *Faust*. *Contempo* by John and Ruth Vassos satirized America of the 1920s with dynamic Art Deco illustrations. John Vassos also illustrated editions of *Kubla Khan* by Samuel Taylor Coleridge, and Oscar Wilde's *Salomé* and *The Harlot's House and Other Poems*.

Other American illustrators at this time were John J. A. Murphy, Charles Kassler, Maxmilien Vox, Edward A. Wilson and William Zorach.

French book illustration reached its highest achievement after World War I. This was a stimulus to collectors, and the interest in book collecting and rare bindings was great. A large section of illustrated books was included in the 1925 Paris Exposition. At this time the favorite form of illustration was the woodcut, either in black-and-white, or color. Other techniques included etching, dry point, lithography, or pochoir, a process by which color was produced by a series of stencils. Raoul Dufy, Foujita, Kees van Dongen and many others were producing book illustrations in the 1920s.

*The New Book-Illustration in France* by Léon Pichon was the subject of a special edition of *The Studio*, Winter 1924. M. Pichon reproduced

Bookplates. Rockwell Kent. *From* Rockwell Kentiana *by Carl Zigrosser (New York: Harcourt, Brace & Co., 1933)*

the work of a long list of French artists including George Barbier, Henri Barthélemy, Bellery-Desfontaines, Robert Bonfils, Paul Emile Colin, Maurice Denis, Raoul Dufy, Paul Hermann, Louis Jou, P. Jouvé, Alfred Latour, Marie Laurencin, Constant Lê Breton, Eddy Le Grand, Le Doux Picart and Paul Véra. The deluxe editions of books with any of these illustrations are available at a price, but the cheaper editions that translated the illustrations by mechanical techniques are also collectible.

However, the master of book illustration was François Louis Schmied. Schmied was not only an illustrator; he often produced the book as a whole, from the design of engravings to the design of the leather binding. Schmied's first work was the engraving and adaptation of P. Jouvé's illustrations of Kipling's *Jungle Book* for the Société du Livre Contemporain. This was started before the war, but not completed until 1918. From this time, Schmied began producing art books that have never been equaled. In addition to artistic typography, layout and illustrations in black-and-white or color, Schmied also designed the binding, which was executed by G. Crette in hand-tooled leather and silver with lacquerwork by Jean Dunand.

Chief among Schmied's original illustrations were those done for *Les Climats*, poems by the Comtesse de Noailles; *Légende du Martin Pecheur*, a poem by Rosemonde Gérard; *Les Ballades Françaises*, by Paul Fort; *Les Quatre Lettres de Daphne*, by Alfred de Vigny; *Deux Contes*, by Oscar Wilde; *Le Cantique des Cantiques*; *La Princesse Boudour* (from *The Arabian Nights*); and *Le Livre de la Vérité de Parole* and *Le Paradis Musulman*, by Dr. J. C. Mardrus.

In England Edward Gordon Craig illustrated an edition of *King Lear* with wood-block designs, in 1923.

Eric Gill, Paul Nash, Frank Brangwyn, Clare Leighton, Percy Bliss, John Nash, Ethelbert White and Leon Underwood were other well-known illustrators in England at this time.


## FASHIONS AND STAGE DESIGN

A large group of young French designers found an opportunity to use their talents in the world of fashion, the theater and interior decoration. Foremost among these talented young artists was Erté, a young Russian whose real name was Romain de Tirtoff. Erté had grown up in Saint Petersburg, then a center of theatrical and artistic life. His artistic ability developed early in life and, at the age of eighteen, he was taken to study portrait painting with one of the best painters in Saint Petersburg. The ballet had made an early impression on Erté, and his love of color and the drama attracted him to the field of fashion and stage design. After a year's study of painting, Erté decided to go to Paris, where he enrolled at the Académie Julian, but he remained there only three months. In 1913, Erté obtained a sketching job with Paul Poiret, then the greatest designer of women's clothes. At Poiret's atelier, Erté made drawings for dresses and theatrical costumes for balls, extravaganzas and theatrical productions. His first publicized costume was for the Dutch dancer Mata Hari.

Although it was usually the custom for the designs from Poiret's studio to go out under the name of Poiret, Erté managed to sign his own name. The first appearance of the signature *Erté* in a fashion magazine was in the *Gazette du Bon Ton* in May 1913. Erté remained with Poiret until the outbreak of the war. There was now no call for chic dress designers or theatrical costumers, so Erté moved to Monte Carlo. From here he sold his first cover, entitled "Schéhérazade," to *Harper's Bazaar* in January 1915, and in March, *Harper's* printed the first of a regular series of fashion sketches by Erté. He was in good company since Léon Bakst, Umberto Brunelleschi, Georges Barbier, Etienne Drian and Dulac also contributed illustrations to *Harper's* at this time. Erté also sold drawings to *Vogue* in June, July and August 1916. For fear of losing him, *Harper's Bazaar* signed him to a ten-year exclusive contract and, from January 1915 to December 1936, Erté contributed two-hundred-forty covers and twenty-five hundred drawings to *Harper's Bazaar*. Erté also designed covers and illustrations in the 1920s and 1930s for *L'Illustration, Fémina, Le Galois Artistique, Plaisir de France* and the English journals *The Sketch* and *Illustrated London News*.

It was between 1920 and 1930 that Erté's fame rose to its greatest heights. During this period, he was designing for French revues, Broadway spectaculars and the motion pictures. The meticulous detail of Erté's brushwork, the dreamlike fantasy of his designs and his rich Oriental color are at their best in the designs for the Folies-Bergère, and for such tableaux as *Conte Hindou* in 1922, and *Les Idoles* and *Le Secret du Sphinx* in 1924. New York spectacles at this time included the *Ziegfeld Follies* and *George White's Scandals*, 1922–1929. Among the best of these designs are "The Rivers," "The Seas" and "Silk."

Erté's designs are in the Victoria and Albert Museum in London and the Museum of Modern Art in New York; the entire collection of designs from *Harper's Bazaar* is owned by the Metropolitan Museum of Art in New York. Erté himself retained the originals of the *Harper's Bazaar* covers and his designs for the Folies-Bergère and motion pictures, so that there are few designs available for collectors. Copies of *Gazette du Bon Ton, Harper's Bazaar* and other journals of the period are now collected for their reproduction of the work of Erté and other French illustrators of the period. Although Erté was not represented in the 1925 Paris Exposition a group of his gouache paintings were included in "Les Annees '25" at the Musée des Arts Décoratifs in 1966. There were also groups of gouache paintings by Georges Lepape, A. E. Marty, and Paul Iribe.

While Erté was designing for *Harper's*, Georges Lepape played the same role for *Vogue*. Georges Lepape and Paul Iribe owed their early fame to Poiret. *Les Robes du Paul Poiret* (1908) by Iribe and *Les Choses de Poiret* (1911) by Georges Lepape, each with ten hand–colored plates, are collectors' items today. Lepape designed costumes for a French film, *Phantasmes*, for the ballet *Ethea*, for Pavlova at the Théâtre des Champs–Elysées in 1920 and for a gala evening at the same theater on May 28, 1924. For the collector, there is a small folder, "Costumes de Théâtre Ballet et Divertissements," published by Lucien Vogel, which contains hand-colored drawings for *Le Coup Manqué*, a pantomime ballet presented at the Théâtre de l'Athenée, November 1915, and for *L'Enfantement du Mort, Miracle en pourpre, noir et or* composed by Marcel L'Herbier and presented for the first time in Paris at the Théâtre Edouard VII, April 11, 1919.

Lepape's fashion drawings for Paul Poiret were published in *Gazette du Bon Ton* in 1913, 1914 and 1920–1925. As was the style with French fashion illustrators, the costumes were displayed in settings and given titles. "Les Cerises" shows a figure against a brilliant blue tree dotted with red cherries. "Les Citrons" sets a costume against a faded vermilion ground, and there are baskets of lemons in the foreground. "Au Clair de la Lune" is a print with vivid purples and cerise.

Lepape also designed posters for the theater and fashion shows: "Le Tour d'Europe de Paul Poiret" (1920) and "Soirée de Gala au Théâtre des Champs-Elysées" (1924).

Paul Iribe was another important designer of this group. In 1912/13,

*Conte l'Oriental.* Gouache by Erté, 1920. *Finch College Museum Art Deco Exhibition*

when Iribe was at Martine, he drew innumerable advertisements for Paul Poiret. Iribe also designed for films and became well known as a decorator and designer of furniture. His best–known illustrations were in *Les Robes de Paul Poiret*. This is a small folio with ten hand-colored plates. In 1918, Iribe was invited to Hollywood to design for *Male and Female,* a motion picture that starred Gloria Swanson. Iribe also did color advertisements for lingerie and perfume for *Comoedia Illustré* and *Gazette du Bon Ton.*

George Barbier was one of the best-known French book illustrators of the 1920s. He worked for various magazines, including the *Gazette du Bon Ton,* and illustrated his first book, a work on the Russian dancer Nijinsky, with text by M. F. de Miornandre, during that period. Drawings of Nijinsky, signed E. William Larry (Barbier's pseudonym), also belong to his early period. The Nijinsky book was followed by one on Mme Karsavina by M. Jean Louis Vaudoyer. Then came various albums including *Guirlande des Mois* and *Les Personnages de Comédie,* published by Albert Flament, Paris, 1922. In this latter rare book, Barbier's drawings are translated into color prints by Schmied. Other books were illustrated in the same way or directly from water-colors. Barbier designed the costumes for Maurice Rostand's play *Casanova,* and illustrated the text of *Casanova,* published in 1919, which included twenty-four color plates of scenes and costumes. Barbier followed this with costumes for Edmond Rostand's *La Dernière Nuit de Don Juan;* Glazounov's *Amarilla;* Weber's *L'Invita-tion à la Valse;* Drigo's *Flute Enchantée;* Edwin Justus Mayer's *The Firebrand;* and Leo Fall's operetta, *La Pompadour.* A group of these drawings were collected in a volume, *Vingt-cinq Costumes pour le Théâtre,* with a preface by Edmond Jaloux and published in Paris in 1927 by Camille Bloch & Jules Meynial. In 1928, *Les Fêtes Galantes* by Paul Verlaine, with twenty-one color lithographs by Barbier, was published. George Barbier also illustrated *Manon, Fille Galante* by H. Bataille and A. Flament. For Hollywood he designed the settings for *Monsieur Beaucaire,* starring Rudolph Valentino. Some of Barbier's most magnificent designs were for *Le Tapis Persian,* a revue at the Casino de Paris in 1920. He also designed for the Folies-Bergère. Barbier combined sumptuous costumes with sober settings so that the beauty of the costume would stand out against a dark neutral back-ground. Along with Erté, Lepape and Iribe, Barbier depicted his models in a decorative and unrealistic manner. Many of Barbier's color prints

*Eventails* (Fans). From *Le Bonheur du Jour*. Pochoir illustration by George
Barbier. Paris, circa 1928. *Robert Brown, the Antiques Center of America*

appeared in *Gazette du Bon Ton,* where he illustrated the costumes of Paquin, Worth and Redfern. The color print *Au Jardin des Hespérides* shows a figure wearing an autumn suit against a background of stylized apple trees. The scene of a girl playing "Le Jeu des Grâces" has a blossom tree in the background.

Charles Martin also belonged to the group of illustrators of *Gazette du Bon Ton,* which included André Marty, Pierre Brissaud, Etienne Drian, Raoul Dufy, George Barbier and others. Martin also did drawings for the magazines *Le Rire* and *La Vie Parisienne,* and worked for the fashion magazines *Fémina, Eve, Vogue* and *Vanity Fair.* Martin also designed scenes and costumes, textiles, wallpapers, furniture and perfume bottles, and made posters for Musidora and for Jeanne Pierly. The decorative designer André Groult commissioned Martin to design a series of decorative panels of country amusements. Line drawings by Martin include two rare series of Marcel Astruc's *Mon Cheval, Mes Amis et Mon Amie.* He also designed an album for *Imprimerie* and illustrated Toulet's *Mariage de Don Quichotte.* A pen drawing of Louis XIII and his favorite falcon shows Martin's wit and imagination. His color etchings include those for De Regnier's *Illusion Héroïque de Tito Bassi,* published by La Roseraie, Montesquieu's *Lettres Persanes;* and Mérimée's *Carmen,* which includes thirty-eight color etchings and eight plates in black-and-white.

Pierre Brissaud was another French book illustrator of the 1920s. He belonged to the group that did illustrations for *Gazette du Bon Ton.* He also illustrated the following books by the pochoir process. Among his pochoir books were *Quatre Petites Filles d'Eve,* by Mme Sarazin de Verly; Flaubert's *Madame Bovary;* René Boylesve's *Alcinor* and *L'Enfant à la Balustrade* (the last three published by Le Livre); and *Leçon d'Amour dans un Parc* by Boylesve. Among Brissaud's deluxe editions with color etchings are Balzac's *Eugénie Grandet* and *Le Petit Pierre,* and *La Vie en Fleur* by Anatole France.

Other fashion illustrators included André Marty, Robert Bonfils and Umberto Brunelleschi as well as Etienne Drian who did a series of line illustrations for *Harper's Bazaar* in 1920. The collector would want to include illustrations for *Daphnis et Alcimadure,* Paris, 1926, with color prints by André Marty. There were also many fashion plates by Marty in *Gazette du Bon Ton.* This magazine is a rare collector's item. Not only are there fashion plates, but there are sketches of hats, shoes,

*Fêtes Galantes* (Paul Verlaine). Pochoir illustration by George Barbier, Paris, 1928. *Robert Brown, The Antiques Center of America*

jewelry and hairstyles, and plates of interiors including furniture by Ruhlmann, Jourdain and Sue et Mare.

Umberto Brunelleschi illustrated several books including a large folio *Les Masques et Les Personnages de la Comédie Italienne* with twelve hand-colored plates, 1914; *Scènes Vénitiennes* with twelve color plates, 1919; and *Chansons Arabes*, 1920; *Chansons Arabes* had eight color plates by Brunelleschi, forty vignettes and fifty miniatures by M. Stab. From 1919 to 1921 Brunelleschi was the art editor of a popular art journal *La Guirlande*. Besides directing the artwork of the magazine, Brunelleschi furnished most of the color plates and sketches. The cuts were to illustrate articles that related to the topics of the day. One article discusses the difference between French and American women and another is about jazz, whereas still another discusses dandies. George Barbier, Polack and several other artists also contributed illustrations. *La Guirlande* is now a collector's item. Though it may be difficult to find these magazines intact, separate illustrations can be found in Paris and in New York shops selling old prints or antiques.

The delicate sentimental colored etchings of the French artist Louis Icart were very popular in the 1930s. The subjects of these characteristically French prints were mainly beautiful women either in the nude or in fashionable dresses of the period. The figure of a woman with three wolfhounds was a favorite subject. Nudes included such titles as *Birth of Venus, Serpent and Apple, Love's Awakening, Eve, Venus, Waterfall, Fountain* and *Hop-La*. There were also figures from the opera: Madame Butterfly, Mimi, Mignon, Musetta, Thaïs and Carmen.

Icart etchings were sponsored by the New York Graphic Society, and they became so much the craze that a Louis Icart Society was founded. The etchings were inexpensive when first issued, but they are collectors' items today and prices have mounted accordingly.

An Icart catalogue included the following titles:

| | | |
|---|---|---|
| Printemps | Colombe Blessée | Jean d'Arc |
| Eté | Marchande d'Oiseaux | Salomé |
| Automne | Marchande d'Oranges | Dalila |
| Hiver | Sappho | Werther |
| Perroquet Bleu | Mme Bovary | Monmartre |
| Café Rouge | Cendrillon | Danse Apache |
| Bons Amis | Premières Cerises | Danse Espanole |

| | | |
|---|---|---|
| Sur les Quais | Thaïs | Le Minuet |
| Place Vendôme | Ecoute | Mardi Gras |
| Divan Rose | Regarde | Miss America |
| Alcove Bleu | Duo | Miss California |
| Jeune Mère | Fidélité | Orchids |
| 1830 | Cachette | White Lilies |
| 1930 | Il Pleut Bergère | Smoke |
| Gouter | Ricuse | Golden Veil |
| Petit Déjeuner | Au Clair de la Lune | |
| Boudeuse | Des Crieurs | |

Icart's name is listed with the group of printmakers whose prints were exhibited and sold at a gallery called L'Estampe Artistique at 32 Rue de Provence in the 1920s. The other artists whose prints were on "exposition permanents" included George Barbier, Marcel Bloch, Bernard Boutet de Monvel, Bouy, Gustave Brisgand, Umberto Brunelleschi, Antoine Calbet, Leonetto Cappiello, Jules Chéret, Delize, Jean Descomps, André Devambez, Georges Dola, Jean Dorville, Dubout, Carle Dupont, Eliott, Giuseppe Fabiano, Abel Faire, Fontan, Forain, Emmanuel Fougerat, Henri Gerbault, Grellet, Albert Guillaume, Henri Guydo, Heinard, Hérouard, Hervé, Icart, Itasse, Jarach, Jonas, Kühn, Léandre, Lemaire, Georges Lepape, Leonnec, André Mantelet–Martel, Henri Martin, Mesples, Millière, Henry Mirande, Louis Morin, Mourolin, Mutin, Nain, Maurice Neumont, Peau, Penot, Francisque Poulbot, Prejelan, Georges Redon, Marthe Regnier, Steinlen, Teure, Vallee, Louis Vallet, Wegener and Willette. The sketch at the top of the advertisement of the gallery depicts a girl sitting among flowered pillows looking at a print, and is signed by Brunelleschi.

Many designs were also made for bookplates. Although the majority of bookplates were conventional and conservative, some were in tune with the times. European bookplates, particularly those made in Germany by Karl Michel, Josef Weiss, W. C. Schmidt and Willi Knabe, the designer of Hitler's bookplate, are modern and interesting. Bookplates in Russia were also interesting, and striking designs were made in Belgium and Poland. Bruno da Osimo designed the bookplates for such important Italians as King Victor Emmanuel and Mussolini.

Bookplates were new to Japan in the 1930s. They were block printed in color on Japanese rice paper and offer a fascinating field for the collector.

Motion picture bookplates of the 1920s include ones of Colleen Moore and Rudolph Valentino, but although they offer name collecting, few of the designs have Art Deco interest. However the Krazy Kat motif of Louise Fazenda's bookplate and a design of circles and symbols made for Walter Anthony, man about Hollywood, are Art Deco.

Sheet music and record sleeves of the 1920s and 1930s have a nostalgic appeal. They also often include Art Deco subject matter and design. Among the sheet-music songs that belong to this category are "Mary Lou," 1926, with an illustration of a girl with bobbed hair and decorations of geometric roses; "A Cup of Coffee, a Sandwich and You," 1925, with a flapper illustration on the cover; "Lucky Lindy," published in 1927 with appropriate airplane decorations; "They Satisfy" (Chesterfields) in 1930; Marlene Dietrich, "Song of Songs"; "Short'nin' Bread" and "My Baby Loves to Charleston."

Record sleeves and book jackets are more difficult to find because they are usually discarded, but a careful search might prove rewarding.

Although there are thousands of matchbooks and matchbox label collections, those with an Art Deco theme have not been collected up

Art Deco playing cards, 1930s. *Betty Lipton, The Antiques Center of America*

Art Deco matchbooks, 1930s. *The New-York Historical Society, New York City*

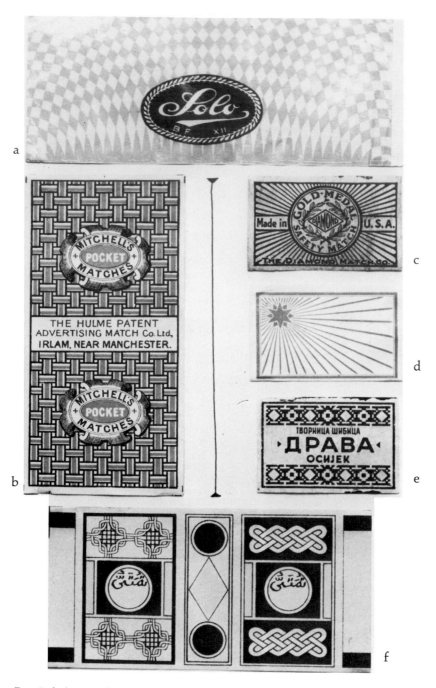

Box Labels. (*a*) Glossy label printed in yellow and orange with dark blue and white medallion, Bernard Furth Factory, Austria. (*b*) British label, black and red on pale yellow. (*c*) American label printed in dark blue on fawn colored paper. (*d*) Swiss label printed in red on yellow paper. (*e*) Yugoslavian label from Osidjek factory, blue on white paper. (*f*) Swedish label by Bryant & May, yellow and dark green on cream paper. *Collection Joan Rendell*

to now. However, there are many designs that fit this category. Match-books and matchbox labels were common to all countries. They were put out by makers of safety matches, such as the Diamond Match Company in America, by makers of cigars and cigarettes, and were also used as advertisements by hotels, restaurants and clubs and to commemorate exhibitions and festivals. A design featuring jazz was on a box made by the Safe Way Matches Ltd. of Sydney, Australia. The Wembley Exhibition in England in 1924 was commemorated on a Swedish "customer's" label. A Russian set of matchbox labels features instruments in an orchestra, and is expressive of the 1920s, as are series made for sports, steamships, and airlines of the 1920s and 1930s. The matchbooks advertising the Chicago World's Fair in 1933 and the New York World's Fair in 1939 are also related to Art Deco.

Many small boxes for powder, gloves, perfume and cigarettes were

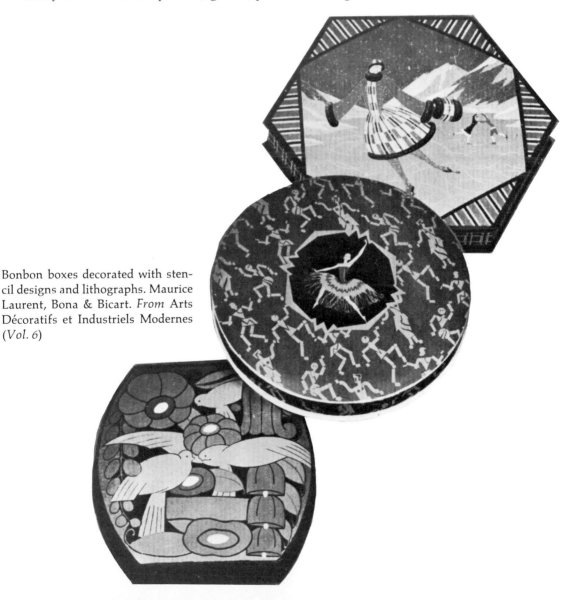

Bonbon boxes decorated with stencil designs and lithographs. Maurice Laurent, Bona & Bicart. *From* Arts Décoratifs et Industriels Modernes (*Vol. 6*)

Fan, powder box, and perfume boxes. Plumereau. *From* Arts Décoratifs et Industriels Modernes (*Vol. 6*)

also covered with painted papers. In the late twenties, the Etablissements Albert Motolet exhibited a group of these colorful boxes, which were designed by various artists, including Maurice Laurent, Nurdin and Germounty. There were many colorful boxes made for the dispensing of perfumes by the various perfume manufacturers, but the most colorful and exotic and the most desirable for the collector today are the rare boxes designed by Poiret and his staff of artists at Martine for his Rosine scents.

Paper fans were also designed at Martine and at other shops, including Primavera; Paul Iribe designed paper fans for Château de Madrid.

A fan advertising "Oxade" was signed by the artist Dorfi. Another fan was made for "La Baule: La plus belle plage d'Europe." These paper advertising fans have red and green dyed frames and are

Fans with mother-of-pearl decoration in geometric designs.
Georges Bastard, Paris. *From* Art et Décoration, *1927*

decorated with brilliant colored scenes and Art Deco motifs. Savonnerie used designs by Robert Bonfils, and Beauvais, those by Bénédictus. Smaller firms used designs by Paul Follot and Sue et Mare.

## BOOKBINDING

The late nineteenth century saw a renaissance of the craft of bookbinding. There were centers of artistic bookbinding in Paris, in Nancy, at the Wiener Werkstätte in Vienna, in Denmark, in Germany and in England. The binders of the Ecole de Nancy at the turn of the century included Victor Prouvé, Camille Martin and René Weiner. In Germany, Leon Gruel depicted a nocturnal scene with a black cat on the binding of *Collected Tales of Edgar Allan Poe*. The interlacing designs of Henry van de Velde were executed by P. Claessens. Josef Hoffmann designed the bindings for the books in Palais Stoclet in Brussels around 1911. Early-twentieth-century bookbinding designers also included Belville, Rapallier and Gustave Dubouchet who worked in Paris. In England, Aubrey Beardsley, M. Lillian Simpson and Sarah T. Prideaux were designing in Art Nouveau style.

As the century advanced, bookbindings became more decorative and designers sought to harmonize them with the content of the book. No longer was fine bookbinding predominantly brown, somber green or deep blue or crimson. Inlays of colored leathers now included lemon yellow, pink, rosy mauve, cobalt blue, jade green and black. Silver, platinum and gold were used in tooling, and panels of lacquer, shagreen and inlays of ivory, metal and wood contrasted with the calf or morocco.

There were many fine bookbindings made in Art Deco style. The designs are usually floral and leaf or Cubist-inspired geometric designs. The most celebrated bookbinder designer in Paris in the 1920s was Pierre Legrain. His designs were executed by the binders Canape, Nouhlac and René Kieffer. In collaboration with René Kieffer he opened a bookbinding studio in 1922. Legrain's designs are in geometric style with parallel lines and concentric circles or conventional foliage. The designs of Kieffer, Georges Cretté, Noulhac and Canape were figurative and floral. Robert Bonfils designed romantic and

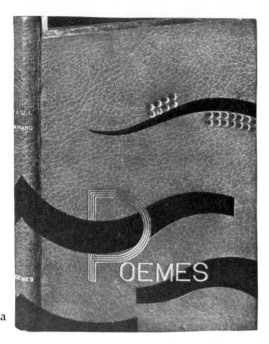
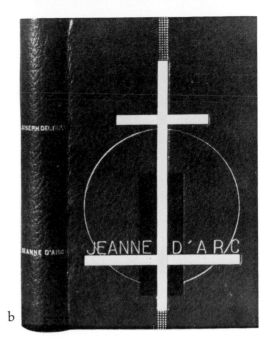

a

b

(a) Bookbinding of pink morocco and black mosaic with letters traced in gold. Pierre Legrain. (b) Bookbinding of cobalt blue morocco and black mosaic with cross of inlaid ivory, and gold letters. Pierre Legrain. *From* Modern French Decorative Arts, *Léon Deshairs*

Bookbindings. Robert Bonfils. *From* Art et Décoration, *1929*

Bookbinding designs by Paul Bonet. *From* Art et Décoration, *1928*

Bookbinding of metalwork and gilt for Fort's *Les Ballades Françaises: Montagne, Forêt, Plaine, Mer.* Paul Fort, 1933. *Finch College Museum Art Deco Exhibition. Binding Paul Bonet*

Bookbinding. *Bottom left:* Geneviève de Léotard. *Bottom right:* green morocco and black mosaic with gold tooling and white edged with silver; horizontal band is of pale gray mosaic. Pierre Legrain. *From* Modern French Decorative Arts, *Léon Deshairs*

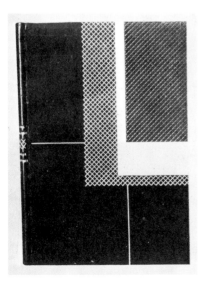

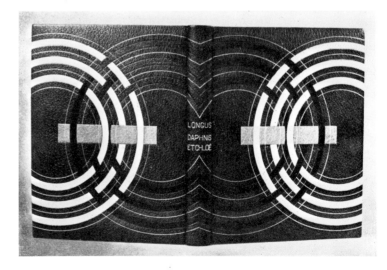

decorative bindings with masks and heads. A binding by André Mare for Poinsot's *Le Foie des Yeux* shows the use of his characteristic geometric rose. Geometric flowers are also used in the binding for Mardrus's *Le Paradis Musulman* illustrated by F. L. Schmied. Paul Bonet was a Cubist-inspired binder. His binding of De Gourmont's *Couleurs* is a combination of slanted lines and interlacing circles, and in the binding for Paul Fort's *Les Ballades Françaises: Montagne, Forêt, Plaine, Mer* he combines his design with metalwork by P. Bout.

Lacquerwork by Jean Dunand is combined with leather on the bindings of several books illustrated by F. L. Schmied, including *Les Climats* by the Comtesse de Noailles. A striking plastic hand is incorporated by Greusevault in the binding for *Le Livre de la Vérité de Parole* by Mardrus.

J. E. Wimmer was a bookbinder connected with the Wiener Werkstätte in the 1920s, and Danish bookbinders at this time included Niels Petersen, Jens Thurslund, Joachim Skovgaard and Ernst Hansen.

There were also a great many women bookbinders in the 1920s, foremost of whom was Rose Adler whose bindings in brilliant colors of leather with inlaid cubist designs of silver and black attracted attention at the many exhibitions of bookbindings. Geneviève de Léotard also designed in the Cubist manner. Her bindings are of colored calf with plain and gold tooling. Other French women bookbinders in the 1920s include Jeanne Langrand, Suzanne Roussy, Mlle de Felice and Yvonne Ollivier.

Collecting Art Deco bookbindings is an expensive hobby, and fine bindings can only be found in established book dealers' shops. For those with smaller purses there are many fascinating book jackets.

## ART DECO POSTERS

One of the most widespread and popular collectors' items today is the poster. This interest is evidenced by the fact that the Museum of Modern Art in New York has held thirty-five poster exhibitions since 1933 and the museum's collection includes two thousand posters. Although there were few posters as such before the mid-nineteenth

*Chemin de Fer du Nord, Nord Express.* Poster by A. M. Cassandre, 1927.
Collection, The Museum of Modern Art, New York. Gift of French National
Railways

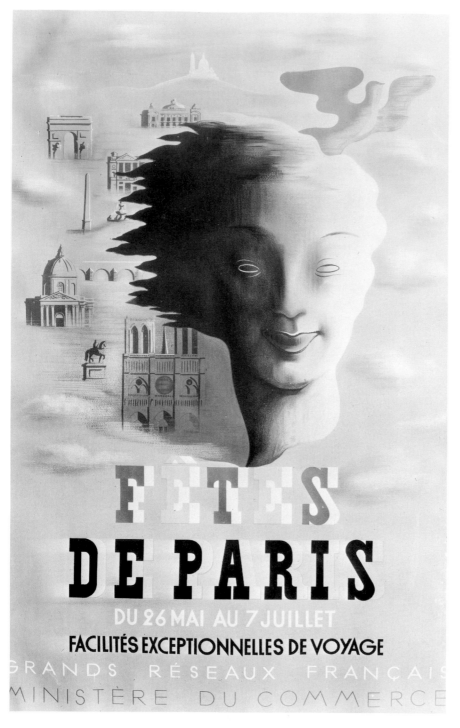

*Fêtes de Paris.* Poster by A. M. Cassandre, 1935. Collection, *The Museum of Modern Art, New York*

century, by the end of the century posters were common to all European countries and to America. Posters of a sort have existed since the time of the Egyptians, and perhaps more than any other art form, reflect the daily life and values of people.

Poster collecting comprises many different categories. Sports posters depict bicycle and horse racing, skating, skiing, tennis, football, basketball, golf and yachting. Transportation is another important poster subject; and the automobile, ship, railroad and airplane are depicted in this category. Among the many interesting posters in this division are those by Cassandre for the railroad Nord Express. There are also posters that advertise foods, fashions, gasoline and automobile tires, cigarettes, cigars and beauty products. But by far the largest category and the most interesting posters are those connected with entertainment. Theater, motion picture and circus posters list names of actors long since dead and plays and theaters no longer in existence. Circus posters with scenes of the ring, the parade and the old circus wagons and animals have a special appeal for many collectors.

In the seventeenth and eighteenth centuries posters were used as propaganda, but the poster as we know it today did not take its form until the nineteenth century. In 1866, Jules Chéret opened his own printing firm and in 1867 he produced a poster for Sarah Bernhardt. From the 1880s, when Toulouse-Lautrec and other well-known artists revolutionized poster design, to the present day, posters have occupied a place between fine art and commercial art.

The decade between 1890 and 1900 was a golden era for the poster. Chéret, Mucha, Cazals and Guillaume were working in France; Aubrey Beardsley, and the Beggarstaff brothers in England; Eugène Grasset and Théophile Steinlen in Switzerland; Frank Stuck in Germany and Cappiello and Bernard in Belgium. As early as 1892 Eugène Grasset became interested in poster design. Grasset, an architect and designer, was influential in the Art Nouveau movement, and his posters for the shop A la Place Clichy and le théâtre de l'Odéon are in Art Nouveau style, as were the posters of Georges de Feure, and the Dutchman Jan Toorop, Alphonse Mucha and Toulouse-Lautrec. The posters of Toulouse-Lautrec, Steinlen and Forain tend toward Expressionism. Also at this time the Japanese print was an important influence in poster design and helped establish the element of clear-cut simplicity. Fauvism, Cubism and the other art expressions of the era are also

*Accélération*. Poster by Paul Colin for Peugeot, 1935. *Collection, The Museum of Modern Art, New York. Gift of Bernard Dairs*

a

b

(*a*) *Gourmandise.* Poster by Jean Carlu. (*b*) *Coquetterie.* Poster by Loupot.
*From* Art et Décoration, *1929*

*Nazimova in Oscar Wilde's "Salomé." Lithograph by Eugene Gise, 1922. Collection, The Museum of Modern Art, New York. Gift of United Artists Corp.*

reflected in poster art. The Viennese geometric style with its elimination of detail and lack of sentiment are seen in posters of Julius Klinger and Richard Teschner (circa 1912 and 1913), which belong to Art Deco. The later posters of Cappiello are also in the modern idiom.

After the war, life took on new dimensions. A new mood grew up with sights and sounds in a new pattern, and the poster artists were among the first to respond to the jazz and frivolities of the postwar twenties. Such poster artists as Cassandre, Roger Perot, C. Kiffer and others expressed the new modified Cubism of Art Deco style with its bold silhouette-type designs, and Bauhaus lettering often avoiding capitals. These clear-cut contrasts of forms and colors had now replaced the arabesque patterns of earlier poster design. Sven Brasch and Bogelund of Denmark designed posters that typified this trend. Bogelund's Tivoli poster with its nervous angularity and abandon expresses the spirit of Art Deco in both style and content. Another especially striking poster was Cassandre's *Etoile du Nord* (1927). At the 1925 Paris Exposition Cassandre had won the *grand prix* for his posters. Other French poster artists of the 1920s included Charles Loupot, who made posters advertising the Voisin car and for the *Exposition des Arts Décoratifs* (1925). Jean Dupas, Delis, Michel Bouchard and Pico were other well-known French poster designers of the 1920s. Pico's poster for the Folies-Bergère is a good example of Art Deco cubism. Paul Colin designed posters for the Théâtre des Champs-Elysées and for Josephine Baker (1925) and the "Nuit du Théâtre à Luna Park" (1928). Between 1922 and 1930 René Vincent made poster designs for Bon Marché, Philips Radio and Voisin automobile company. André E. Marty and Georges Lepape, Charles Dufresne, Herbin, Gesmar and André L'hote designed posters for the theater and other types of amusement. Well-known theatrical posters include those of Maurice Chevalier by C. Kiffer (1923) and Mistinguette by C. Gesmar (1922). In 1923 Jean d'Yien designed his striking poster for Shell gasoline. It was first published in Paris, but later adapted for English use. The leaping figure of a horse is set against a black background.

In Germany, Walter Gropius, the genius of the Bauhaus, gave new aspects to poster design, and Bauhaus lettering became the style for poster work in the 1920s. Interesting German posters were made by Frank Stuck, Bernhard Rosen, Hinklein, and Bauhaus artists Moholy-Nagy, Josef Albers, Joost Schmidt and Oskar Schlemmer. A cubist face dominates the *Reklame Schau* poster of Bernhard Rosen.

Cartoon for theatre mural. Watercolor on paper. Alfred Tulk, 1931. *Lent by
Stanley Insler, for the Finch College Museum Art Deco Exhibition*

Well-known poster artists of Italy working in the Art Deco style include Lazza and Codognato. Codognato's striking poster for the Fiat automobile was made in 1925.

In England, a majority of the postwar posters advertised the London Omnibus and Electric Underground (subway). The best-known designer of these Underground posters was F. C. Herrick. Other designers who made posters for the Underground in the 1920s include Frank Brangwyn, Elijah Cox, Lionel Edwards, Aubrey Hammond, George Sheringham, Rex Whistler and E. McKnight Kauffer. Kauffer's designs were based on Cubism, and the best known ones were the new cover of *The Studio* magazine (1929), the Fire of London design for the London Museum (1922) and the Derry and Toms winter sale poster (1920). Posters by Ashley Havinden also show Cubist influence.

Many English posters also display the English interest in humorous advertising which resembled cartoons. Posters by John Hassall, Will Owen and Henry A. Harris were popular humorous posters of the 1920s.

The earliest American poster designers were Louis Rhead, Will Bradley, Maxfield Parrish, William Penfield, Joseph C. Leyendecker and Charles B. Falls. Other American poster designers of the 1920s and 1930s include James Preston, Louis Fancher, Samuel N. Abbott, J. E. Sheridan, William H. Taylor, James H. Daugherty, Ethel Reed and Florence Lundborg. Rockwell Kent designed posters for the Carnegie Institute International Show, the Convalescent Relief Committee of Bellevue Hospital Exhibition, the Art patrons of America Show and Books for the Home.

One of the most popular categories of poster collecting is the art poster. In the 1930s, such artists as Chagall, Matisse, Braque and Miró made posters that can be classified as art posters. In America few art posters were available until recent years. The first American art posters were made for the Lincoln Center for the Performing Arts in 1960. Art galleries and museums had artists design posters for their own shows. A few years ago a concern called Poster Originals began publishing and distributing art posters. Seventy-five posters by American artists were produced in the 1950s and 1960s, many of them are in Art Deco style especially those of Roy Lichtenstein, Milton Glaser, Richard Lindner and Frank Stella.

Art Deco posters are now in great demand, and their prices are rising accordingly. If the collector is interested in a particular designer, there are many signed posters to choose from, and these naturally bring a higher price. However, there are many posters of the period that are valuable for their design, even though they are not signed and the maker is not known. The type of design and the subject matter will help to determine the date.

# 11 JEWELRY, COMPACTS, PURSES AND CIGARETTE LIGHTERS

PARIS WAS THE FASHION CENTER FOR JEWELRY THROUGHOUT THE NINETEENTH century and into the twentieth as it was for clothes and furniture and the decorative arts. In the early 1900s René Lalique was a designer of jewelry. He began to use crystal and enamel in novel colors and shapes rather than depending on precious stones, and his designs were different from any that had come before. The approach to jewelry design was thus changed, and from that time on, what counted was beauty and craftsmanship rather than cost and carats. Lalique revolutionized jewelry and brought decorative jewelry into style, yet his designs remained traditional. At the same time that Lalique was fashioning dragonflies, lizards, swans and women with flowing tresses in Art Nouveau style, the designers of Germany and Austria were producing geometrical and abstract jewelry. Koloman Moser and the other designers of the Wiener Werkstätte made decorative jewelry in beautiful forms using silver materials and semiprecious stones such as coral, agate, opal, turquoise, lapis lazuli and moonstone. Sometimes, precious stones were also placed in a sharply angular geometric framework. However, it was the baskets of flowers and carved crystal plaques

Crystal brooch with faceted glass stones and nude spring maidens. René Lalique, circa 1920. *Finch College Museum Art Deco Exhibition*

Brooch with flower-basket motif. Platinum with diamonds, carved emeralds, rubies and sapphires. Circa 1925. *Finch College Museum Art Deco Exhibition*

introduced by Lalique that were so stylish in France for many years. Even after 1920, when they were no longer the height of style, they remained a favorite with many people. Cartier, too, designed many brooches with baskets of flowers and doves at this time. Baskets of flowers and horns of plenty, which were used in the designs of chair backs and textiles in the early 1920s, were seen in jewelry with diamonds, emeralds and rubies. Mauboussin designed brooches with baskets of fruit and fountain motifs. The Egyptian influence was seen in scarab pins and bracelets. Egyptian motifs were also used in a bracelet of rubies, emeralds and sapphires made by Boucheron.

Later in the twenties the jewelry became bolder and simpler in design and reflected the influence of the Orient. Such materials and stones as black onyx, crystal, jade and coral became the fashion, and colored enamels were used as settings for jewels. Heavy circular brooches, link bracelets and pendants, tassels of seed pearl and long hanging earrings became the style. Under the influence of Cubism, jewelry became simpler in design, and shapes became triangular, hexagonal and trapezoidal to go with modern furnishings and costumes. Cubism, Futurism and Mondrian and de Stijl, Klee and the Bauhaus, all had an influence on jewelry design, and through these various sources, jewelry acquired a new stylistic language.

By the 1920s the geometric trend had caught on with the public. Pforzheim, Germany, which was the birthplace of geometric jewelry,

Pin of blue Egyptian faience with smoky topaz scarab, emeralds, diamonds, and gold and black enamel. *Lent by Jon Nicholas Streep, for the Finch College Museum Art Deco Exhibition*

Bracelet of Egyptian motifs with rubies, emeralds and sapphires. Boucheron, Paris. *Parke-Bernet Sale Catalogue, April 6, 1960*

Necklace. Six-strand onyx and coral bead torsade with a sixteen-strand tassel. Circa 1923. *Finch College Museum Art Deco Exhibition*

became the center for such designs. Decorative jewelry, with semi-precious stones used alone or combined with diamonds or other precious stones, became the craze. Some of the best-known goldsmiths working at Pforzheim in the 1930s included Kurt Baer, Fritz Stabler, Kurt Heinzelmann, Wilhelm Oehler, Adolf Schüler, Zunft Turm, Erwin Holzle, Erwin Murle, Zunft Jungkunst and Armin Zweigenthal.

Not only the choice of materials and the geometric designs but also the manner of construction and the way gems were cut showed the influence of the modern mode. Long narrow baguette cuttings

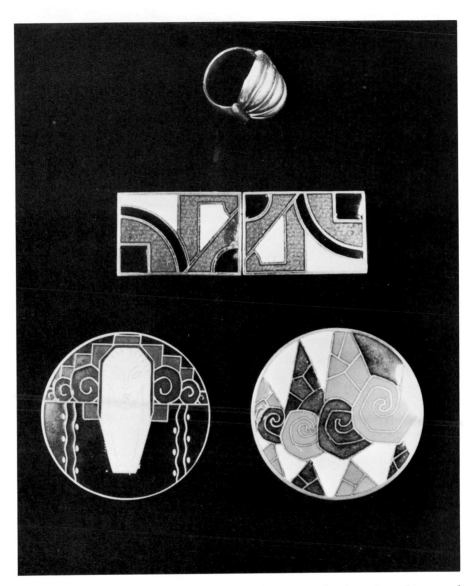

Art Deco ring, rectangular belt buckle, and two circular brooches. *Barry and Audrey Friedman, The Antiques Center of America*

simplified lines and textures. Other stones were cut in convex
cabochon shapes and polished, but not faceted. Squares, circles, triangles and rectangles were used in combinations in designs for rings,
brooches and so on. A fluted pattern imitating organ pipes was carried
out in gems, gold, silver or platinum. Large gems were often mounted
in invisible settings. In 1925 the most important Paris designers in
this style were Jean and Georges Fouquet, Raymond Templier,
Boucheron, Mauboussin, Vever, Dusansoy, Linzeler et Marchak,
Chaveton Frères, Gardey, August Bonaz, Lacloche, Charles Mellerio,
and Gérard Sandoz. Between 1925 and 1937 the list also included the
following designers or jewelers: Paul Brandt, René Robert, Mlle

Rectangular-shaped brooch with diamonds. Platinum with a hanging vine
motif of carved emeralds, rubies, sapphires and diamonds. Circa 1925. *Finch
College Museum Art Deco Exhibition*

Cigarette cases with lacquer designs. Raymond Templier. *From* Art et Décoration, *1930*

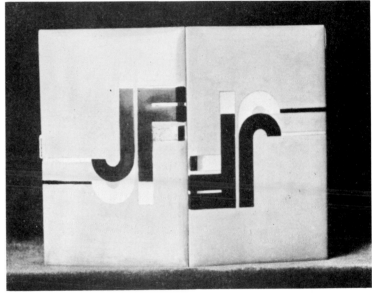

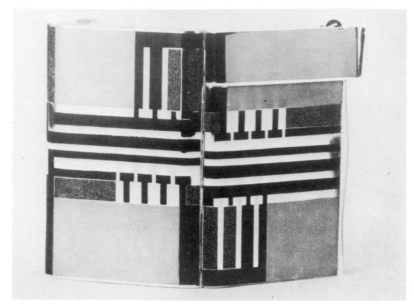

a

b

(*a*) Cigarette case of enamel and silver, Gérard Sandoz. (*b*) Cigarette case,
Raymond Templier. *From* Art et Décoration, *1929*

Toussaint for Cartier, Bray, Chaumet, Regner, Van Cleef & Arpels, Filos, Herz-Belperron, Fulco di Verdura, Mme Antoine Boivin, Eugène Schlumberger and Harry Winston.

In the exhibition "Les Années '25," jewelry by Georges and Jean Fouquet was shown. There were pendants of crystal, lacquer, coral and rose diamonds, gold and onyx. A triangular brooch made in 1923 was composed of ivory, turquoise, onyx, and brilliants. Another brooch consisting of two half disks was of "or gris et onyx." Rings were of gold and onyx.

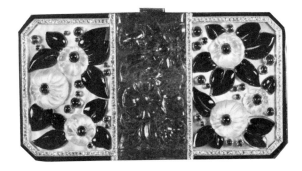

Vanity case of gold and platinum. Black enamel with carved lapis lazuli plaque, moonstones, sapphires, diamonds, and mother-of-pearl. Circa 1928. Van Cleef & Arpels, Paris. *Finch College Museum Art Deco Exhibition*

Oval frosted glass medallion and white-gold pendant with coral, agate, moonstone, and onyx set in cubistic design. Jean Fouquet, 1925 Paris Exposition. *Finch College Museum Art Deco Exhibition*

An article in the American magazine *Jewelers' Circular*, February 21, 1929, describes the new modernistic jewelry design with its "flair for the geometric and the use of dynamic symmetry." The article goes on to say: "This new manner is well exemplified in some of the latest brooch designs. These jewels are gaining in popularity with their wider use. They have outgrown their single usefulness as corsage ornaments and now appear worn on the shoulder, as girdle fastenings, hat trimmings, buckles for the gloves and the slippers and fastenings for the back of the dress." Illustrated was a brooch with huge carved jade ovals placed at either end of the design and diamonds grouped to make the central detail. By the thirties these angular designs had once and for all replaced the earlier, more traditional forms of Art Deco jewelry.

Germany has always been known for fine goldsmith work. Emil Lettré was one of the best-known German goldsmiths of the 1920s. He made brooches and pendants of enamel, diamonds, pearls and emeralds in bold modern designs. Theodor Wende of Pforzheim was also a designer of rings, pendants and brooches in the modern geometric style. In Berlin, Josef Wilm was known for his fine gold jewelry; his designs included pendants of masked faces. Hand-hammered jewelry of silver, enamel and semiprecious stones was very much the vogue in the late 1920s and 1930s in Germany. Munich was an important center for this type of jewelry. The best-known goldsmiths making this type of jewelry included Max Olofs, Eugen Sherer, Max Obletter, L. Bub, Lorenz Durner and Franz Valentin. They loved coral, and it was combined with both gold and silver in brooches, link bracelets and pendants. Lorenz Durner made cubistic zodiac designs in enamel and metal. Long earrings and bracelets were made of silver and smooth semiprecious stones, whereas bracelets, rings and cigarette cases were made of silver studded with coral. Karl Rothmuller, who was formerly a goldsmith to the Bavarian Court, made fine jewelry of gold, coral, jade, and black enamel, as well as signet rings with lapis lazuli seals. Ivory carved in cubistic designs was also popular. Emmy Zweybrück-Prochaska designed and made many ivory pendants. Dagobert Peche and Josef Hoffmann made silver pendants in typical angular Wiener Werkstätte designs. Many pendants with cut-out cubistic designs were made for P. Bruckmann & Söhne by various designers, including Edward Hopf, Carl Beyeren, Friedrich Schmid-Riegel, Robert Huttl, Karl Wahl, Gerta Schroeder and Josef Michel

Lock. Gold jewelry of excellent workmanship was made at Schwäbish Gmünd by Fritz Möhler, Karl Miller, Ewald Muller and Julius Vetter. Heavy square and rectangular settings were set with large stones of coral, moonstone, tourmaline and pearls. The stones were contrasted with colored enamels and fine patterns of gold granulation. Similar jewelry was also made in Sweden by Wiwen Wilson, and in England by H. G. Murphy.

Psuedo-barbaric jewelry became the fad in the thirties. But one of the most important developments in jewelry design came about when artists and sculptors began designing pendants, brooches, rings and bracelets. The important artists who interested themselves in jewelry design included Braque, Cocteau, Arp, Man Ray, Max Ernst, Dali, Dubuffet, Picasso, Calder, Giacometti, Afro, Fontana and Gio Pomodoro. The jewelry has the artist's signature along with that of the maker.

In the late 1920s when it became the style to wear jewelry in the daytime, costume jewelry was made to match the wearer's dress. French couturier Coco Chanel is credited with having made artificial jewelry fashionable. A long necklace of crystals set in silver or white metal was a favorite accessory in the 1920s. The designs again followed the lead of the decorative arts, which by now had accepted the ziggurat, the triangle, the cone and chrome tubing. Silver and chrome beads and brilliants replaced the precious stones of fine jewels. Such designers as Jean Desprès made costume jewelry of gold,

Necklace and pendant in silver and ivory. Jean Desprès, 1937. *Lent by Galerie Sonnabend, for the Finch College Museum Art Deco Exhibition*

Cigarette case of black lacquer with coquille d'œuf. *Lent by Lillian Nassau, Ltd., for the Finch College Museum Art Deco Exhibition*

Compact of lapis lazuli and enamel. French. *Parke-Bernet Sale Catalogue, December 11, 1969*

enamel, turquoise and ivory. Jean Dunand and C. Fauré also made costume jewelry of glass enamel and lacquer in coquille-d'oeuf finish. Cigarette cases and compacts were also made in matching designs. This type of costume jewelry was never cheap, although, of course, it was less expensive than jewelry of precious stones.

Mass produced costume jewelry was made of artificial materials such as Bakelite and various types of plastics. Aluminum disks were set with imitation onyx and colored enamels. These were sold at prices within the reach of all. The designs were poor and the colors gaudy, but they pleased the public for whom they were made. The French jewelry makers, Marlene, Movado, Murat and Pomone, made this type of jewelry, and they also made cigarette cases, powder boxes and compacts of enamel and silver or chrome with geometric Art Deco designs.

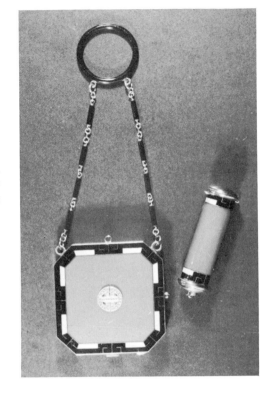

Vanity case and lipstick of rose diamonds, platinum, and enamel. Circa 1927. *Lent by Jon Nicholas Streep, for the Finch College Museum Art Deco Exhibition*

Compact and lipstick of gold and enamel with geometric rose design. *Parke-Bernet Sale Catalogue, December 11, 1969*

Cigarette case of silver and gold. Paul Flato,
circa 1925. *Lent by Jon Nicholas Streep, for
the Finch College Museum Art Deco Exhibition*

Mesh purses. *Left:* Estelle Mushabac for
Whiting & Davis. *Center and right: Julie
Kelter, The Antiques Center of America*

Cigarette case of jade and lapis lazuli.
*Parke-Bernet Sale Catalogue, December
11, 1969*

Group of mesh purses with Art Deco designs. Circa 1929. *Julie Kelter, The Antiques Center of America*

*No. 4023-BT*
*Inspired by Paul Poiret*
Enameled Petite Armor Mesh Costume
Bag of bouffante pouch-shape, modern-
istic frame 5 inches wide, with silver
finish—a new Paul Poiret model.
**Price $18.00**
*Subject to Keystone Discounts*
*Order Through Your Wholesaler*

Mr. C. A. Whiting
*CABLED*
from Paris :

*"Announce new*

# PAUL POIRET POUCH-SHAPE
# COSTUME BAGS *June 1st"*

Again Whiting & Davis Company has the newest
idea in Costume Bags ready and waiting for the
trade well in advance of the mode! Always in
step with advance news from the Paris salons—
always hand in hand with Fashion!

The new POUCH-SHAPE Costume Bags, inspired
by Paul Poiret, are ready now in Armor, Petite
Armor and Dresden Enameled Mesh.

This trade-mark is
stamped on the frame
of every genuine Whit-
ing & Davis Costume
Bag. It is the hall-mark
of excellence and stands
for more than 50 years
of creative craftsman-
ship.

# *Whiting & Davis Co.*

*World's Largest Manufacturers of Costume Bags*
*Makers of Costume Jewelry for Everyone*
**Plainville (Norfolk County), Mass.**
**In Canada: Sherbrooke, Quebec**

New York:                                    Chicago: F. E. Whiting
366 Fifth Ave.                               31 N. State St.

Advertisement for mesh purses made by Paul Poiret for Whiting & Davis.
*From* The Jewelers' Circular, *June 6, 1929*

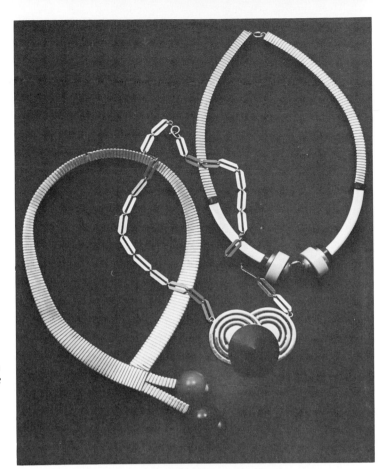

Chrome and Bakelite necklaces.
*Barry and Audrey Friedman, The*
*Antiques Center of America*

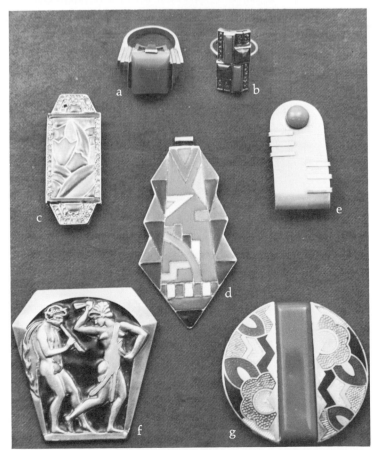

(*a*) Silver and chalcedony ring.
(*b*) Silver, lapis lazuli, coral, and
marcasite ring. (*c*) Silver, enamel,
and rhinestone brooch. (*d*) *Géo-*
*métrie.* Enamel pendant. (*e*) Silver and coral tie clasp. (*f*) Brooch,
enamel on copper, F. Bouillot,
Paris. (*g*) Enamel and Bakelite
buckle. *Barry and Audrey Fried-*
*man, The Antiques Center of*
*America*

Compacts and boxes of black, red, green and orange enamel. Circa 1935. *Robert Morgan and Frank Weston, The Antiques Center of America*

# 12 KITSCH

KITSCH IS CHARACTERIZED BY POOR DESIGN, CHEAP MATERIALS, UGLY, IN-harmonious color and shoddy workmanship. In other words, kitsch is bad taste. It was produced to appeal to the lowest popular taste. Garden gnomes and plaster replicas of Greek statues and the saints, the Eiffel Tower pepper grinder, Turkish brass slippers with colored glass beads, wooden and brass leg nutcrackers and erotic corkscrew figures of the Mannekin Pis are all kitsch.

The word "kitsch" was originally in use only in the German language and, in the German dictionary, *kitsch* is defined as trash. The word entered English usage some years ago and was employed to describe art of debased quality. Harold Rosenberg defines kitsch as the debasement of refined design in popular adaption. Although every period of art and every category of collecting has its kitsch form, Gillo Dorfles in his book, *Kitsch* (1969), considers kitsch as mainly limited to our age, and he believes that it was brought about by the advent of the machine, which made it possible to produce and reproduce pseudo-art objects. Hermann Broch ties kitsch to the sentimentalism and romanticism of the nineteenth century and suggests that it should be called the century of kitsch instead of the century of romanticism.

Beginning with the 1920s, kitsch and daily life became inseparable. Kitsch art reflected the thoughts and life of the average person of the time. The language of Art Deco kitsch produced in the 1920s and 1930s is that of the masses and gives a better picture of the popular taste that any other art form of the era. It is a record of events rather than of abstract theories or movements, and its motifs are drawn from life. Art Deco in its higher form was influenced by Futurism, Fauvism, Cubism and other art movements of the era whereas Art Deco kitsch drew its inspiration from everyday life and pictured life itself. The motifs of Art Deco kitsch are the top hat of the dandy; the flapper with bobbed hair and short skirts; black jazz musicians with banjo, saxophone and accordion; dice and cards; cocktail shakers and cocktail glasses; the Charleston and black-bottom dancers. In stylized form, these motifs are seen on glass and pottery ashtrays, silver and enamel compacts and lighters, and on plastic souvenirs with the Eiffel Tower scrambled together with bubbles and Café de Paris nudes.

Each article of Art Deco has its kitsch, or trashy, form, from sculpture, china and glass cigarette cases, bookends, ashtrays and cheap plastic jewelry to an alabaster figure of a harem dancer or a vase made to represent a pack of cards.

Pottery. *Left:* dice bottle, French. *Center:* cup of cards with devil handle. *Right:* teapot with grotesque face. *Fred Silberman, The Antiques Center of America*

Art Deco kitsch is now the craze. Most collectors today concentrate on this type of Art Deco because it is cheap and because it is fun. They ignore its bad taste and cheap quality and collect it just as other collectors concentrate on beer trays, Jim Beam and Avon bottles and many other popular antiques. This is due in part to nostalgia, but the alliance between Art Deco and Pop Art is the basis of the interest of those collectors who are too young to remember the time when Art Deco was new. Although most Art Deco kitsch articles have no intrinsic value, they are living history. They help to round out a picture of the age and are often intimate and eloquent souvenirs of a bygone era. Bookends and ashtrays are the most fertile field for the collector of Art Deco kitsch. Those of pottery and cheap metal are the most available. The gypsy teakettle, twin girls holding a crystal snowball, a figure of Cleopatra, are some of the subjects. There are also pottery figures dancing the tango, cocktail shakers in the shape of the Jolly Friar, dancing bears, plaster heads showing different hairstyles and hats, and teapots in the form of racing cars. The

Two figures of girls with greyhounds on leash. *Left:* Plaster of Paris figure, painted. *Right:* metal overlaid with colored plaster, signed P. Manfred. *Betty Lipton, The Antiques Center of America*

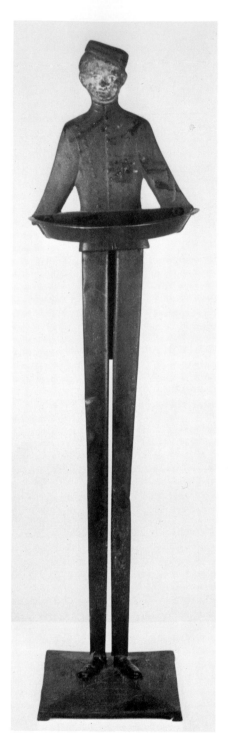

Tall bellboy ashtray of cast iron. *Betty Lipton, The Antiques Center of America*

Cheap pottery with popular themes: ashtray of girl with bare legs and exposed breasts; vase of nude in shower; vase of girl sitting on crescent moon. *Betty Lipton, The Antiques Center of America*

Egyptian sphinx was a popular subject for bookends. Then there is the erotic side of Art Deco kitsch that includes pottery ashtrays with nudes whose bulging bosoms are sometimes lit up by light globes. There are also cheap pottery figures of Leda and the Swan, and its variation Leda and a Pelican.

The exhibition, "Les Années '25" at the Musée des Arts Décoratifs in 1966, produced a twofold effect depending upon one's age. To some, it recalled an era of pleasurable memories of trips on the *Ile-de-France;* of *Harper's Bazaar* covers by Erté; of the extravaganzas of Ziegfeld and *George White's Scandals*—to which we are bound by

Satyr child riding a grasshopper. Colored pottery, signed F. V. Hohmannhofer. *Fred Silberman, The Antiques Center of America*

nostalgia. The exhibition also brought about a revival of the Art Deco style, which began to take hold on posters, book jackets and fashions in dress fabrics. Musicals of the thirties were revived on the Broadway stage, and television productions began to display jagged geometric sunrays, and rainbows. Magazine covers and advertisements took on Bauhaus typography, and architectural preservation societies reexamined the architecture of the 1920s and 1930s.

Artists including Roy Lichtenstein, Frank Stella, Peter Blake and Milton Glaser have exploited the vulgar side of the art of the 1920s and 1930s, and are incorporating the Art Deco motifs and themes in their paintings. They have made the phony side of Art Deco the high art of the 1970s. It is campy and entertaining.

A group of huge gaudy clay figures by Patti W. Bauer shown at the Museum of Contemporary Crafts in New York City draws on Art Deco for its theme and colors. Enormous lips, bare legs, wheels and checkerboards in gaudy pinks, reds, oranges and luster are served with such appropriate names as *Ketchup Kiss, Moondog Dream* and *Unchilled Lips Flavored with Lady Fingers.* In the same exhibition, William Warehall serves up kitsch slices of gooey cake, ice cream sundaes and lobster for the next generation of collectors.

*Ketchup Kiss.* Pottery figure of luster and red, pink, black and blue glazes. *Patti W. Bauer. Museum of Contemporary Crafts*

# BIBLIOGRAPHY

## PERIODICALS

*Art et Décoration.* Librairie Centrale des Beaux-Arts, Paris, 1897 to date.
*Mobilier et Décoration.* Edition Edmond Honoré, 1920 to date. Sevrès.
*Art et Industrie.* Paris, 1922–1935.
*L'Art Vivant.* Librairie Larousse, Paris, London, 1925–1938.
*The Studio Yearbook of Decorative Art.* The Studio, London, 1906–1932.
*Deutsche Kunst und Dekoration.* Alexander Koch, Darmstadt Verlagsanstalt, 1897–1934.
*Dekorative Kunst.* F. Bruckmann A.G., München, 1898–1929.
*Jewelers' Circular.* Philadelphia, 1900–1930.

## EXHIBITION CATALOGUES

Les Années '25. Art Deco/Bauhaus/Stijl/Esprit Nouveau, Musée des Arts Décoratifs, Paris, 1966.
Art Deco. Finch College Museum of Art, New York, 1970.
The World of Art Deco. The Minneapolis Institute of Arts, 1971.
Posters by A. M. Cassandre. The Museum of Modern Art, New York, 1936.

## BOOKS

*Album de l'Exposition Internationale des Arts Décoratifs.* Edité par *l'Art Vivant.* Paris: Librairie Larousse, 1925.

ARWAS, VICTOR. *Art Deco Sculpture*. New York: St. Martin's Press, 1984.

BATTERSBY, MARTIN. *The Decorative Twenties*. New York: Walker & Co., 1969.

BRUNHAMMER, YVONNE. *The Nineteen-Twenties Style*. London: Paul Hamlyn, 1959.

CAMARD, FLORENCE. *Ruhlmann: Master of Art Deco*. New York: Harry N. Abrams, 1984.

CLOUZOT, HENRI. *La Ferronnerie Moderne*. Series 1–5. Paris: Charles Moreau, 1925.

————. *La Ferronnerie Moderne à l'Exposition des Arts Décoratifs*. Paris: Charles Moreau, 1925.

————. *Style Moderne dans la Décoration Interieure*. Paris: Charles Massin, 1926.

DESHAIRS, LEON. *L'Hôtel du Collectionneur*. Paris: Albert Lévy, 1926.

————. *Modern French Decorative Art*. 2 vols. London: The Architectural Press, 1926–1930.

DORFLES, GILLO. *Kitsch*. New York: Universe Books, 1969.

DOWLING, HENRY G. *A Survey of British Decorative Art*. London: F. Lewis Limited, 1935.

DUFRENE, MAURICE. *Ensembles Mobiliers à L'Exposition Internationale de 1925*. Paris: Charles Moreau, 1928.

FOLLOT, PAUL. *Intérieurs Français au Salon des Artistes Décorateurs, 1927*. Paris: Charles Moreau, 1927.

FRANKL, PAUL T. *New Dimensions*. New York: Payson & Clarke, 1928.

JANNEAU, GUILLAUME. *Modern Glass*. London: The Studio, Ltd., 1931.

KAHLE, KATHARINE MORRISON (McClinton). *Modern French Decoration*. New York: G. P. Putnam's Sons, 1930.

McCLINTON, KATHARINE MORRISON. *Introduction to Lalique Glass*. Des Moines: Wallace-Homestead, 1978.

————. *Lalique for Collectors*. New York: Charles Scribner's Sons, 1975.

NAYLOR, GILLIAN. *The Bauhaus*. London: Studio Vista, 1968.

OVERY, PAUL. *De Stijl*. London: Studio Vista, 1969.

PEVSNER, NIKOLAUS. *Pioneers of Modern Design*. London: Pelican, 1960.

PUIFORCAT, JEAN. *Orfèvrerie, Sculpture*. Paris: Flammarion, 1951.

RAPIN, H. *La Sculpture Décorative Moderne*. Paris: Charles Moreau, 1925.

RENDELL, JOAN. *Matchbox Labels*. New York: Frederick A. Praeger, 1968.

SPENCER, CHARLES. *Erté*. New York: Clarkson N. Potter, 1970.

RICKARDS, MAURICE. *Posters of the Twenties*. London: Evelyn, Adams & Mackay, 1968.

VERONESI, GUILIA. *Style and Design: 1909–29*. New York: George Braziller, 1960.

WHITE, PALMER. *Poiret*. New York: Clarkson N. Potter, 1973.

Abbott, Samuel N., 243
Adams, Herbert, 206
Adams & Poole, 117
Adnet, Jean Jacques, 24, 59, 107
Aiken, Robert I., 206
Alavoine, L., 24
Alber, Anni, 69
Albers, Josef, 241
Alesch, Frau von, 71
Altenloh of Brussels
    (silversmith), 164
Altman, B., 37
Anderson, Just, 163
Andirons, wrought iron, *58*
Angelo, Emilio, 188
Angman, Jacob, 164
Applebaum, M., 198
Argy-Rousseau, Gabriel, 4,
    147–48
Armchairs, 27–28, 37, 59, 60
Armor Bronze Co., 202
Art Décoratif (Deco), ix, x, 6-12
    Moderne, ix, 6
    Nouveau, 6–7, 186
*Art et Industrie* (magazine), 124
Aschermann, Edward, 38
Astruc, Marcel, 220
Atelier Primavera, 113
Atomizer, *149*
Au Printemps, *9*, 65, 107, 113
Aubusson, 69

B. Altman. *See* Altman, B.
Baccarat, 137, 150
Baer, Kurt, 248
Bagge, Eric, 71
Bags, ladies', 74
Bagues Frères, 53
Bakst, Léon, 7, 215
Ballroom design, *92*
Barbier, George, 215, 218
Barraclough, Gladys, 69
Barrias, Louis, 186
Barron, Phyllis, 71
Barthélemy, L., 186
Bauer, Patti W., 269
Bauhaus, 7, 33, 59, 69, 247
Beach, Chester, 188, 189, 206
Béal, Georges, 135–37
Beardsley, Aubrey, 230, 237
Beauvais, 69
Beds, 33
Behrens, Peter, 165
Bel Geddes, Norman, 207
Bénédictus, Edouard, 61, 65
Bergh, Elis, 148

Bernadotte, Sigvard, 163
Bernard Rice & Sons, 178
Berthold, Karl, 165
Bertsh, Karl, 35
Beyer, Liz, 69
Beyeren, Carl, 254
Bianchini-Férier, 62
Bigelow Carpet Co., 71
Billings, Henry, 42
Binder, Wilhelm, 165
Bing & Grondahl, 109
Binns, C. F., 118
Blake, Peter, 269
Blanc, Pierre, 124
Bliss, Percy, 214
Block, Hans, 170
Block, Lucienne, 147
Bogelund, 241
Boin-Taburet (silversmith), 160
Boivin, Antoine, 253
Bojesen, Jai, 163
Bon Marché, 9
Bonbon boxes, 227
Bonet, Paul, 234
Bonfils, Robert, 7, 62, 109, 220,
    230, 234
Bonnard, 104
Bonza, August, 250
Book
    illustrations, 211 ff.
    jackets, 234
Bookbinding, 230 ff.
Bookends, *201*
Bookplates, *213*, 223
Borglum, Gutzon, 188
Bottles, *125*
Bouchard, Michel, 241
Bouché, Louis, 42
Boucheron, 247, 250
Bouix, Lucien, 65
Bouraine, Marcel, 187
Bourdelle, Antoine, 81
Bout, P., 234
Bowls, *105*, *139*, *151*
Box labels, *226*
Bracelets, *247*
Bradley, Will, 243
Brandt, Edgar, 11, 50, 53, 74, 81,
    93, 97, 131
Brandt, Paul, 250
Brangwyn, Frank, 116, 214, 243
Braque, Georges, 7, 243
Brasch, 241
Bray, 253
Brenner, Victor D., 205
Breuer, Marcel, 59

Breuhaus, Fritz A., 35, 37
Brindeau, Paul, 83
Brissaud, Pierre, 220
Broch, Hermann, 263
Bronze
    bookends, *190*
    figures, *187–97*
    inkwells, *186*
    medallions, 203 ff.
    statuettes, 188 ff.
    vases, *178*
Brooches, *246*, *250*
Bruckmann, P., & Söhne, 165, 254
Bruhns, Da Silva, 9, 66
Brunelleschi, Umberto, 215, 220,
    222
Brunet, Meunie et Cie, 62, 65
Brychta, Jaroslav, 150
Bub, L., 254
Burch-Korrodi, Meinrad, 170
Buthaud, René, 4, 104

Cabinets, 30, 37
Caldwell, J. E., 86
Candlesticks, 131, *175*
Candy boxes, 120
Capon Frères, 83
Cappiello, 237, 241
Carder, Frederick, 147, 148
Cardheilhac (silversmiths), 159
Carpets, 67, 68, 73, 74
Carter, Pat, *136*
Cartier, 88, 90, 246, 250
Cassandre, A. M., 237, 241
Cazaux, 137
Ceramics, 103 ff.
Chabert-Dupont, Mme., 74
Chagall, Marc, 243
Chairs, 27–28, 35, 37, 59
Chalon, Louis, 186
Chambellan, René, 39
Chandeliers, 91
Chanel, Coco, 255
Charder (designer), 146
Chareau, Pierre, 7, 10, 20, 28, 59
Chaumet, 253
Chauvin, Jean, 124
Chéret, Jules, 237
Chermayeff, Serge, 49
Cheuret, Albert, 86
Chevalier, Georges, 137, 150
Christofle (silvermakers), 159
Chrysler Building, 4
Church silver, 170
Cigarette cases, 158, 250–52, 256,
    288

Claessens, P., 230
Clark, Allan, 188, 189
Clarke, Harry, 71
Cliff, Clarice, 116, 117
Clocks, 81 ff.
    bronze, 82
    chrome, 84
    crystal, 90
    enamel, 89
    glass, 84, 85
    with intarsia decoration, 87
    lacquer, 88
    marble, 82, 83
    porcelain, 86
    silver, 86, 89
Codognato, 243
Coffee services, 123
Colenbrander, 110
Colin, Paul, 241
Commode, 30
Compacts, 256, 257, 262
Compagnie des Arts Français
    (Sue et Mare), 9, 17
Confitures, 120
Conkling, Mabel, 188, 189
Console, wrought iron, 52, 55
Coty, 131
Coulon, Marthe, 124
Courtebassis, Jean, 124
Cox, Elijah, 243
Cox, George C., 119
Craig, Edward Gordon, 214
Crette, G., 214
Crocker, Templeton, 22
Cros, Henri Isidore, 146–47
Crystal
    bottles, 155
    plate, 136
Cubism, 7
Cumming, Rose, 38
Cuzner, Bernard, 170

Dallin, Cyrus E., 188, 190
Dammouse, Albert, 147
Dampt, Jean-August, 186
Danish silversmiths, 163
Daugherty, James H., 243
Daum, Antoine, 4, 11, 85, 94, 97,
    137, 146
Daum Brothers, 140
Daurat, Maurice, 159
David, Fernand, 109
De Stijl, 69, 247
De Lettrez (perfume bottle
    designer), 150
Decoeur, Emile, 4, 103
Décoration Intérieure Moderne
    (DIM), 9, 66, 69
Décorchemont, François, 4, 137, 148

Delaunay, Sonia, 62
Delblassé, 135–37
Delis, 241
Delvaux, 144
Derain, André, 7
Deshairs, Léon, 10
Deskey, Donald, 38, 39, 71
Desks, 30
Desprès, Jean, 160, 255
Despreti, George, 147
Des Vallières, Georges, 7, 17
Deutsche Kunst (magazine), 12,
    33
Diamond Match Co., 227
Die Kunst (magazine), 12, 33
Dishes, 134, 179
Djo-bourgeois, Elise, 10, 20, 28,
    59, 62
Dodge, Frank E., 188
Doilies, 74
Dominique, 24, 30, 57
Dongen, Kees van, 213
Doors, lacquer, 54
Doorway, wrought iron, 51
Dorfles, Gillo, 263
Dorn, Marion, 71
D'Orsay, 150
Doucet, Jules, 66
Drapery materials, 69
Drésa, André, 7, 62
Drian, Etienne, 215, 220
Dubois, Gaston, 159
Dubouchet, Gustave, 230
Dufrène, Maurice, 9, 10, 17, 28,
    29, 57, 61, 65, 81, 107, 160
Dufresne, Charles, 17, 241
Dufy, Jean, 107, 108
Dufy, Raoul, 23, 62, 69, 107, 109,
    213, 220
Dumas, Paul; 65
Dumoulin, Georges, 137, 140
Dunand, Jean, 4, 11, 83, 178–79,
    234, 256
Dunhill, Alfred, 187
Dupas, Jean, 241
Durner, Loren, 254
Dusansaoy (jewelry designer),
    250

Eberle, Abastenia, 188
Edwards, Lionel, 243
Ehlers, Jetta, 118
Elgin-American Mfg. Co., 178,
    182
Embroidery
    designs, 71
    on organdy, 78
    picture, 79
    pillows, 76

    tablecloth, 77
Enamel
    bowl, 172
    boxes, 172
    objects, 140
    vases, 182
Erté (Romain de Tirtoff), 9, 10
    214–19, 267
Eterna Lighters, 182
Etling, 135–37
Exposition des Arts Décoratifs,
    ix, 6–8, 10, 50, 59
Exposition Internationale des
    Arts Décoratifs et Industriels
    Moderne. See Exposition des
    Arts Décoratifs

Fabric design, 63, 64, 65
Faguays, P. le, 187
Falls, Charles B., 243
Fancher, Louis, 243
Fans, 228, 229
Fashion, 214
Fauré, C. (glass designer), 4, 181,
    256
Feure, Georges de, 237
Figures, 265, 266, 268, 269
    bronze, 97
    ceramic, 108
    glass, 127, 131, 150
    metal, 98
    porcelain, 111, 121
Filos, 253
Fire screens, wrought iron, 52, 57
Fisker, Kay, 163
Fjerdingstad, Christian, 159
Flanagan, John, 206
Foley Potteries, 117
Follot, Paul, 9, 10, 17, 61, 65, 81,
    116
Foltin, Willi, 35, 37
Fontaine, Anne Marie, 65
Fontan, Suzanne, 65
Forain, 237
Fostoria Glass Co., 148
Foujita, 23, 62, 213
Fouquet, Georges, 250, 253
Fouquet, Jean, 11, 250, 253
Foxton, W., Ltd., 69
Francisci, Anthony de, 206
Frank, Jean-Michel, 22
Frankart, 97
Frankl, Paul, 9, 38
Fraser, James Earle, 206
Fraser, Laura Gardin, 188, 206
Frechet, André, 24
French, Daniel Chester, 206
Fressinet, 65
Friedleander Co., 198

Friedmann, E., 170
Friesz, E. Othon, 104
Frismuth, Harriet W., 188, 190
Fuchs, Emil, 188, 189
Fuller, Loie, 187
Furniture, 13–60
    American, 37–42
    armchairs, 27–28, 37
    beds, 33
    British, 49
    cabinets, 30, 37
    chairs, 27–28, 35, 37
    commode, 30
    desks, 30
    German, 35–37
    ironwork, 50–57
    metal, 50–60
    rationalist, 20–23
    sidechairs, 28
    sofas, 29
    tables, 30, 53
    traditionalist, 13–18
    tubular, 59
    wrought iron, 50–57

Gabriel, René, 24, 65
Galeries Lafayette, 9, 17, 62, 65
Gallerey (clock designer), 81
Gauguin, Jean, 109
Garcelon, Adrien, 62
Gatelet, Hélène, 107
Gauchet-Guillard, Madame, 9
Gauvenet, M., 81
Genet & Michon, 97, 137
Geometric jewelry, 247
German silversmiths, 165
Gesmar, 241
Gill, Eric, 173, 214
Glaser, Milton, 243, 269
Glass, 127ff.
    blown glass figures, 150
    box, 142
    candlesticks, 131
    Czech, 149–50
    decorative panels, 131
    enameled, 144
    figures, 127, 135, 136, 138, 153
    in jewelry, 127
    knife rests, 132
    lamps and lighting fixtures, 131
    Pâte-de-Verre, 146–48
    perfume bottles, 131–34, 150, 154
    radiator caps, 132, 133
    seal stamps, 132
    vases, 144, 146
Gleadowe, R. M. Y., 170
Gobelins (tapestry), 69
Godden, Geoffrey A., 117

Gorham, 176, 188
Goupy, Marcel, 83, 108, 137
Granger, Mme G., 135–37
Grasset, Eugène, 237
Griesser, Paul, 35
Gris, Juan, 7
Gropius, Walter, 241
Gross, Fritz, 35, 37
Groult, André, 9, 18, 65, 150, 220
Gruel, Leon, 230
Gruppe, Karl, 188
Gueden, Colette, 65, 107
Guénot, Auguste, 109
Guerlain (perfume), 154
Guiguichen, Suzanne, 62
Guillaume (designer), 237
Guiraud-Rivière, Maurice, 124, 192

Hall, Marian, 38
Hammond, Aubrey, 243
Hansen, Ernst, 234
Harris, Henry A., 243
Hassall, John, 243
Haviland, Theodore, 107, 108
Heal, Sir Ambrose, 49
Heckmann, Albert, 119
Heinzelmann, Kurt, 248
Herbin, 241
Herbst, René, 10, 22, 28, 33, 62
Herrick, F. C., 243
Herz-Belperron, 253
Hiesz, Géza, 135–37
Hinklein, 241
Hirsch, J. B., 202
Hlava, Pavel, 149
Hoffmann, Josef, 4, 7, 33, 35, 37, 110, 148, 165, 182, 230, 254
Holzle Erwin, 248
Hopf, Edward, 254
Horter, Earl, 176
Hughes, Graham, 165
Hunebelle, André, 85, 94, 137
Huntington, Anna Hyatt, 188, 190
Huttl, Robert, 254

Illustration, book, 211ff.
Incense burners, 123
International Exhibition of Art in Industry, 37
International Silver Co., 176
Iribe, Paul, 7, 23, 216, 218, 228
Ironwork furniture, 50
    fireplace equipment, 57
    tables, 53
Ivory, 198
Ivory and bronze figure, 195

Jallot, Léon, 10, 14, 81
James Powell and Sons.
    See Powell, James, and Sons
Janusch Mfg. Co., 202
Jaquemin, 194
Jaulmes, Gustave, 17, 69, 109
Jeannert, Pierre, 24, 59
Jensen, Georg, 163
Jewelry, 261
Jewett, Maude S., 188
Johnson, Bernard P., 188
Joubert, René, 9, 24
Joubert et Petit, 66
Jourdain, Francis, 7, 10, 33, 107
Jouvé, P., 214
Jungkunst, Zunft, 248
Jungnick, Hedwig, 69

Karasz, Ilonka, 71
Kassler, Charles, 213
Kauffer, E. McKnight, 71, 243
Kent, Rockwell, 176, 211, 213, 243
Kieffer, René, 230
Kiffer, C., 241
Kilham, Teresa, 71
Kirk, Arthur Nevill, 173
Kiss, Paul, 53, 81
Klee, Paul, 69, 247
Klinger, Julius, 241
Knabe, Willi, 223
Knife rests, 132
Kohlmann, Etienne, 9, 10, 23, 33
Konti, Isidore, 188
Kosta, Glasbruk, 148
Krop, Hildo, 110
Kyhn, Kund, 109

Labels, matchbox, 224, 227
Lace, 71, 75
Lachaise, Gaston, 127
Lacloche, 250
Lacquer, eggshell, 179
Lalique, René, 4, 10, 33, 91, 93, 94, 97, 127–35, 245–46
    candlesticks, 131
    decorative glass panels, 131
    glass clocks, 85
    glass factory, 134–35
    glass figurines, 127
    influence of, 137
    jewelry designs, 127
    knife rests, 132
    lamps and lighting fixtures, 131
    molded opalescent glass, 135
    perfume bottles, 131–34, 150, 154
    radiator caps, 132, 133
    vase, 135, 136
Lalique, Suzanne, 62, 108, 109

knife rests, 132
lamps and lighting fixtures, 131
  molded opalescent glass, 135
  perfume bottles, 131–34, 150,
    154
  radiator caps, 132
  vase, 135
Lalique, Suzanne, 62, 108, 109
Lallemand, Robert, 96, 107, 119
Lamps, 91 ff., 201
  bronze, 94, 96, 97
  crystal, 95
  with figures, 97, 98, 99, 100
  floor, 100, 101, 102
  glass, 95
  wrought iron, 93
Langrand, Jeanne, 234
Lanooy, Chr., 110
Laparra, 4, 160
Larcher, Dorothy, 71
Läuger, Max, 113
Laurencin, Marie, 7, 18, 65
Laurent, Georges, 124, 187
Laurent, Maurice, 228
Lavergne, Jeanne, 124
Laville, Pierre, 96, 119
Lawrie, Lee, 206
Lazza, 243
Le Corbusier, 24, 33, 59
Le Faguays. See Faguays
Le Verrier, Max, 198–99, 201
Leach, Bernard, 116
Léger, Fernand, 66
Legrain, Pierre, 8, 230
Legras, 146
Leighton, Clare, 214
Leleu, Jules Emile, 24, 37
Lenoble, Emile, 4, 103, 104
Leon, Paul M., 123
Leonard, Agathon, 186, 187
Léotard, Geneviève de, 234
Lepape, Georges, 216, 218, 241
Lescaze, William, 38
Lettre, Emil, 165, 254
Leyendecker, Joseph C., 243
Lhote, André, 241
Lichtenstein, Roy, 243, 269
Lightblau, Ernst, 170
Lighting fixtures, 91 ff., 98
  wrought iron, 94
Lindner, Richard, 243
Linossier, Claudius, 4, 179
Linzeler, 250
Lion-Cachet, 110
Liqueur bottles, 120
Liquor sets, 120–23
Llaurerson, Laurert, 163
Lobmeyer, J. and L., 149
Lock, Josef Michel, 254–55

Löffer, B., 110
Loos, Adolf, 7
Lord & Taylor, 37, 71
Louis Icart Society, 222
Loupot, Charles, 241
Louvre, 9
Luce, Jean, 4, 144
Lundborg, Florence, 243
Lunn, Dora, 117
Lurçat, Jean, 69
Lutyens, Robert, 49

Mabru, Raoul, 123, 124
Macintosh, Charles Rennie, 7, 156
McKenzie, Robert Tait, 188
MacLeary, Bonnie, 188, 189
McLeish, Minnie, 69
MacNiel, Hermon A., 206
Macy, R. H., 37, 71
Magne, H. M., 123
Mahias, Robert, 62
Maison Martine, 14, 23, 33, 61,
    62, 65
Maîtrise, La (at Galeries
    Lafayette), 9
Mallet-Stevens, Robert, 7, 33, 59,
    66
Mandalian Manufacturing Co.,
    182
Manship, Paul, 187, 206
Manzana-Pissarro (son of
    Camille Pissarro), 69
Marchak, 250
Mare, André, 9, 17, 62, 150, 234
Marinot, Maurice, 4, 11, 17, 137,
    140, 141, 142–43, 150
Martel Brothers, 109
Martin, Camille, 230
Martin, Charles, 220
Martin, Henri, 124
Marty, André E., 216, 220, 241
Matchbooks, 223, 225, 227
Matet, Maurice, 9, 24, 59
Matisse, Henri, 7, 104, 243
Mauboussin (silver designer),
    246, 250
Mayodon, Jean, 4, 103, 104
Mayrhofer, Adolf von, 165
Medallic Art Co., 205, 207
Medallion(s), 253
  American, 205
  bronze, 203 ff
Meire, Hildreth, 39
Meissen, 86
Mellerio, Charles, 250
Menhuis, Bert., 110
Mesh purses, 289
Metal furniture, 50
  fireplace equipment, 57

tables, 53
tubular, 59
Metthey, André, 103, 104
Mexican art, 8–9
Meyfarth, Marianne, 110
Michel, Karl, 223
Midwinter, W. R., 117
Mies van der Rohe, Ludwig, 24,
    59
Miller, Karl, 255
Mina-Loy, Mme, 96
Minneapolis Institute of Art, 3
Miró, Joan, 243
Mobilier et Décoration
    (magazine), 91 ff.
Mohler, Fritz (silversmith), 255
Moholy-Nagy, 241
Molyneux (dress designer), 150
Mondrian, Piet, 69, 247
Moser, Koloman, 33, 110, 165,
    245
Motolet, Albert, 228
Movado (designer), 256
Mucha, Alphonse, 237
Muller, Ewald, 255
Müller Frères, 94
Murat (jewelry maker), 256
Murle, Erwin, 248
Murphy, Harry, 170, 255
Murphy, John J. A., 213
Murray, Keith, 116
Murray, Staite, 116
Musée des Arts Décoratifs, 3
Musée Galliera, 81
Mushabac, Estelle, 288
Mustard pots, 120

Nash, John, 214
Nash, Paul, 71, 214
Nathan (designer), 109
Navarre, Henri, 4, 85, 137, 140
Necklaces, 248, 255, 261
New Book-Illustration in France,
    The (Pichon), 219
New York Graphic Society, 222
Newcomb pottery, 118
Newport pottery, 116
Nics Frères, 53
Nielsen, Harald, 163
Nielsen, Kay, 109
Nude figure, 139, 145

Obletter, Max, 254
Oehler, Wilhelm, 248
Ollivier, Yvonne, 234
Olofs, Max, 254
Orrefors Factory, 148
Osimo, Bruno da, 223
Otte, Benita, 69

Owen, Will, 243

Panels, decorative glass, 131
Papiers Peints de France, 65
Parnell, Gwendolen, 117
Parr, Harry, 117
Parrish, Maxfield, 243
Parsons, Edith B., 188, 189
Pâte-de-Verre glass, 146–48
Patout, Pierre, 33
Paul, Bruno, 33, 35, 37
Pearson, Ralph H., 71, 211
Peche, Dagobert, 4, 33, 71, 148,
    165, 182, 254
Penfield, William, 243
Perfume bottles, 131–34, 150, 154,
    *154, 228*
Perot, Roger, 241
Perret (architect), 7
Perriand, Charlotte, 24, 33, 59
Peruvian art, 9
Petersen, Niels, 234
Pforzheim, 248, 254
Picasso, Pablo, 7, 69, 104
Pichon, Léon, 213
Pickle pots, 120
Pico (designer), 241
Pierly, Jeanne, 220
Piguet, Ch., 53
Pillows, embroidered, 76
Pins, *137, 247*
Placques, illuminated, 97
Playing cards, 224
Poillerat, Gilbert, 53
Poiret, Paul, 23, 62, 215
Poisson, Pierre, 57, 109
Pollak, J., 170
Pommier (designer), 109
Pomone (boutique), 9, 256
Pompeiian bronze, 202
Ponti, Gio, 38, 113, 159
Poor, Henry Varnum, 119
Porcelain, 103ff., 120ff.
    figures, *111, 121*
    plate, *112*
    vases, *109, 113, 118*
Posters, 234ff., *235*ff.
Postgate, Margaret, 188
Pottery, 103ff., 114, *264, 267*
Poupelet, 109
Powder box, *228*
Powell, Alfred, 49, 116
Powell, James, and Sons, 148
Powell, Louise, 49, 116
Powolny, M., 110
Preiss, Fritz, 83, *193–94*
Preston, James, 243
Prideaux, Sarah T., 230
Primavera, 9, 107

Print, silkscreen, 72
Proctor, A. Phimster, 188, 190
Proschowski, P., 109
Prouvé, Victor, 230
Prutshcer, Otto, 165
Puiforcat, Jean, 4, 11, 33, 57, 157
Purses, mesh, 182, *260*
Putnam, Brenda, 206

R. H. Macy. *See* Macy, R. H.
Radiator caps, 132, 133
Radio City Music Hall, 4, 39–42
Ramsden, Omar, 173
Rancati (rug designer), 71
Rapin, Henri, 24, 131
Ravenscourt pottery, 117
Record sleeves, 224
Redon, Odilon, 104
Reed, Ethel, 243
Reeves, Ruth, 42, 71
Regner, 253
Reiss, Henriette, 71
Reiss, Winold, 71
Renard, Marcel, 107, 205
Rhead, Louis, 243
Ricci, Nina, 131, 132, 154
Richards, Lucy C., 188
Riemerschmid, Richard, 165
Rings, *249*
Rivir, A., 160
Robert, René, 250
Robineau, Adelaide Alsop, 118
Robj, 4, 96, 120, 123
Rodhe, Johan, 163
Rodicr, 9, 65, 74
Rogers Bros., 176
Rönnebeck, Arnold, 110
Ronson Corp., 182
Rosen, Bernhard, 241
Rosenthal, 110
Roth, Marianne, 149
Rothmuller, Karl, 254
Rottenberg, Ena, 149
Roussy, Suzanne, 234
Rouard, Géo, 83, 104, 107, 108
Rouault, Georges, 104
Royal Doulton, 116
Royal Porcelain Manufactory,
    109
Royal Staffordshire, 117
Rugs, 65, *67, 68,* 73, 74
Ruhlmann, Emile-Jacques, 10, 11,
    18, 30, 33, 57, 61, 65, 94, 109
Russell, Sir Gordon, 49, 148
Rustic Well Foundry, 202

Saarinen, Eliel, 8, 38, 173
Sabino, 85, 93, 94, 97, 137, 144–46
Safe Way Matches Ltd., 227

Saint-Gaudens, Augustus, 205
Salons des Artistes Décoratifs 10,
    24
Sandoz, Gérard, 157, 250
Saponaro, 113
Scent bottles. *See* Perfume Bottles
Schenck, Edward, 53
Schillinger, Joseph, 71
Schlemmer, Oscar, 241
Schlumberger, Eugene, 253
Schmid-Riegel, Friedrich, 254
Schmidt, Ernst, 165
Schmidt, Joost, 241
Schmidt, W. C., 223
Schmied, François Louis, 214, 234
Schneider, 147, 148
Schoen, Eugen, 38
Schröder, Alexander, 37
Schroeder, Gerta, 254
Schuler, Adolf, 248
Sculpture
    bronze, 202
    figure, 185
    miniature, 198
Seal stamps, 132
Sears, Philip, 188
Sefton & Co., 69
Seguy, 62
Selmersheim, 81
Sendé, 150
Serré, Georges, 103, 104
Serrjère, Jean, 109, 157, 159
Sevin, Lucille, 135–37
Sèvres, 86, *86,* 107, 109, 124, 147
Sheet music, 224
Sherer, Eugen, 254
Sheridan, J. E., 243
Sheringham, George, 71, 243
Side chairs, 28
Silk fabric designs, *63, 64*
Silkscreen print, 72
Silver, *158, 160*
    basket, *167*
    bowl, *161*
    box, *164, 168–69*
    candelabra, *159*
    candlesticks, *173*
    church, 170
    cigarette boxes, *174*
    cup, *159*
    dish, *161*
    goblet, *167*
    hot water jug, *166*
    saucer, *159*
    sugar bowl, *162*
    table service, *161*
    tea and coffee service, *170*
    tea sets, *161, 164, 167, 174*
    tobacco boxes, *169*

tray, *163*
sculpture, *171*
vases, *158, 160, 173, 174, 175,*
    *179*
Silverplate tea set, *176*
Silversmiths
    Danish, 163
    German, 165
Simmern, Henri, 103, 104
Simon, Mario, 23
Simpson, M. Lillian, 230
Skarica, Fini, 74
Skovgaard, Joachim, 234
Societé Française de Papiers
    Peints, 65
Societé Richard-Ginori, 113
Society of Medalists, 208
Sofas, 29
Sognot, Louis, 24
Solon, Leon V., 119
Sotheby's, 146, 147
Soubinin, Seraphin, 179
Sougez, Madeleine, 107
Spencer's, S. S., Sons, 202
Stab, M., 222
Stabler, Fritz, 248
Stabler, Harold, 117, 170, 173
Stabler, Phoebe, 117
Stage design, 214
Stark, J. Dugald, 49
Stark Bros., 49
Stehli Silk Corporation, 71
Steichen, Edward, 71
Steinlen, Theophile, 237
Stella, Frank, 243, 269
Stephany (fabric designer), 62,
    65, 66
Steuben crystal, *149*
Steuben Glass Co., 147, 148
Stolzi, Gunta, 69
Straumer, Heinrich, 35
Stuart, 148
Stuck, Frank, 237, 241
*Studio Yearbook of Decorative
    Art, The,* 124, 148, 150
Subes, Raymond, 11, 33, 50, 53,
    81, 83
Sue, Louis, 17, 57, 62, 65
Sue et Mare (Compagnie des Arts
    Français), 9, 10, 17, 28, 29, 33,
    65, 150, 160
Sullivan, Louis, 7
Sutherland, Graham, 117, 148
Symonds, R. W., 49
Syosset pottery, 119
Szabo, 83

Tables, 30
    ironwork, 53

wrought iron, *56*
Tablecloths, 69, 74, 77, *80*
Tapestries, 65, 69, *70*
Taylor, William H., 243
Tea cozies, 74
Teague, Walter Dorwin, 38, 71,
    148
Tea services, 123ff.
Templier, Raymond, 33, 150, 151,
    250, 252
Tereszizuk, P., 186
Teschner, Richard, 241
Textiles, 61, 71
Thieck, Francis, 123
Thonet, 24, 59
Thurslund, Jens, 234
Tiffany Co., 176
Toorup, Jan, 237
Toulgoust, Pierre, 124
Toulouse-Lautrec, Henri, 237
Toussaint, Mlle, 253
Treskow, Elizabeth, 165
Turin, Pierre, 205
Turm, Zunft, 248

Underwood, Leon, 214
Upholstery materials, 69
Urban, Joseph, 38

Valentin, Franz, 254
Val-Saint Laurent, 148
Valtat, Louis, 104
Van Cleef and Arpels, 253
Van der Sluys, C., 110
Van Doesburg, Theo, 69
Vanity case, *253, 257*
Vases, *128, 129, 130, 136, 137, 141,*
    *142, 143, 147, 151, 179, 180,*
    *181, 184*
    porcelain, *109, 113, 118*
    pottery, *104, 106, 107*
    stoneware, *104, 105*
    wrought iron, *55*
Vassos, John, 211
Veit, Friederich, 170
Velde, Henry Van de, 156 230
Véra, Paul, 17, 62, 69
Verdura, Fulco di, 253
Vetter, Julius, 255
Vetter, Lilli, 74
Vever (fabric designer), 250
Viard Glassworks, 140
Vibert, Max, 69
Victoria Picard & Co., 178
Vincent, René, 241
Vinegar bottles, 120
Vlaminck, Maurice de, 104
Vox, Maxmilien, 213
Voysey, Charles A., 7
Vuillard, Edouard, 104

Vuitton, Gaston Louis, 150
Vyse, Charles, 117

Waals, Peter, 49
Wagner, Otto, 7
Wahl, Karl, 254
Wallpaper, *66*
Walter, Aleric, 147
Ward, Lynd, 211, 213
Warehall, William, 269
Waring & Gillow, 71
Weber, Kem, 38, 173
Wedgwood, 116
Weiner, René, 230
Weiss, Josef, 223
Wende, Theodor, 165, 254
Whiltshaw & Robinson, 117
Whistler, Rex, 243
White, Ethelbert, 214
Whiting & Davis, 182
Wiener Werkstätte, 4, 6, 23, 33,
    71, 110, 119, 149, 150, *167,*
    245
Wieselthier, Vally, 113
Wilcox Silver Plate Co., 176
Wilkinson pottery, 117
Wilm, Josef, 165, 254
Wilm, Michael, 165
Wilson, Edward A., 176, 213
Wilson, Elsie Cobb, 38
Wilson, Wiwen, 255
Wilton carpets, 71
Wimmer, J. E., 234
Winston, Harry, 253
Winter, Ezra, 42
Wolfers, Phillippe, 164, 186
Wolfers Frères, 164
Wood carving, *212*
Wright, Frank Lloyd, 7, 38
Wrought iron
    andirons, *58*
    console, *52, 55*
    doorway, *51*
    fireplace equipment, *52, 57, 57*
    furniture, *50*
    lamps, *93*
    lighting fixture, *94*
    tables, *53, 56*
    vase, *55*

Yates, Julie Nichols, 188
Yien, Jean d,' 241
Young, Mahonri, 188, 190

Zack, Léon, 150
Zahour, V., 149
Zorach, William, 42, 213
Zweigenthal, Armin, 248
Zweybruck-Prochaska, Emma, 254